Travels with My Son:

Journeys of the Heart

BY LAURA NOE

TRAVELS WITH MY SON

Copyright © 2014 by Laura Noe

All rights reserved. No part of this publication may be reproduced, stored in or introduced into a retrieval system, or transmitted in any form, or by any means (electronic, mechanical, recording, or otherwise), except as may be expressly permitted by the applicable copyright statutes or without the prior written permission of the Publisher.

Printed in the United States of America
ISBN-13: 978-0-9884523-8-1
First Edition: August 2014
Library of Congress Control Number: 2014938054

Cover design by Martin Lopez
Cover photo by Abdellatif Chakir
Inside photos by Laura Noe and Hilliard Hudson Wolfe

The author is alone is solely responsible for the content of this book and bears all responsibility for any claims arising from the publication of the book.

To My Mother
Dorothy Lucey Noe

July 9, 1936 — October 7, 1990

With a single loving and encouraging word,
she transformed the way I looked at myself
... and the world.

"Go."

It is because of her that I am the verb I am today.
She inspired in me a confidence, love of the world, and belief.
I miss her every day.

Travels with My Son:

Journeys of the Heart

Table of Contents

Preface	Depth	9
Chapter 1	My Mother, Milk Bones, and Marriage	13
Chapter 2	Building Confidence	27
Chapter 3	Connecticut Choices	45
Chapter 4	France	49
Chapter 5	Morocco	63
Chapter 6	Germany	89
Chapter 7	The Czech Republic	97
Chapter 8	Austria	127
Chapter 9	Hungary	137
Chapter 10	Turkey	147
Chapter 11	Food	189
Chapter 12	Coming Home	197
Chapter 13	What Are You?	207
Chapter 14	Citizen of the World	211

PREFACE

Depth

> "We shall not cease from exploration, and the end of all our exploring will be to arrive where we started and know the place for the first time."
> — T.S. Eliot

Travel is one of my life's passions. When I became a mother, my love of learning and travel did not wane — it intensified. I realized that being Hudson's mom was the best and most important job I would ever have. I wanted to infuse in him a love of learning and travel, and ignite a spark of curiosity in him.

I wanted to share my passion for the world with him.

When I started writing about traveling with my son, I took out all of the journals I packed with daily recounts and descriptions of the places we went. Taped next to our penned journal entries, are receipts — for everything, even cans of Coke. Even buying a can of Coke is an experience in places where language and customs differ.

As with any good journey, I went places and learned things. But what I learned about most was myself.

My original intent was to revisit the trips, sharing highlights, recounting what we saw and experienced. But I also had a deeper goal: to show what my son, a white American boy, learned about the world. The writing and retelling of our adventures revealed another story, that of my own journey as a mother and as a woman. The travel was significant for him, but it had a profound effect on me as well.

It's true what they say about kids growing up so fast. I am reminded of that when I look back to our trip to France and the image of 10-year old Hudson on Omaha Beach in Normandy. It feels as if I just took that picture. The bond between mother and son is nothing new. These trips gave us a new closeness. They took me into a deeper part of myself, as well. I realized the significance of time spent together, going beneath the surface of life.

I wanted to share my passion for the world with him. This desire grew as he grew, and our adventures together have made us better people.

As of this writing, we have been to four continents together. We have seen highly gentrified places as well as countries that are less well-marketed. We tend to prefer the grittier places, the less slick, as they feel more authentic. We also prefer to focus on a place and really get to know it. We want to understand its essence, as opposed to hitting a lot of places to cross off our list. We are after depth, knowing, and understanding.

We found the essence of Morocco in the foothills of the Atlas Mountains. If Marrakech is the groovy, hip face of Morocco, then the Berber Village is its soul. Adobe homes were packed tightly onto hard-packed dirt streets. Deep ruts served as gutters. The kids of the Berber Village greeted us with expectation in their eyes. We had a bag of Jolly Ranchers.

We are conscious of being Americans and make an effort to speak quietly. We offer ourselves as ambassadors for our country. We hope to offset the negative stereotypes of phony, lazy, and stupid. Hudson loves it when people approach us and speak anything but English. He loves the anonymity and the surprise when they discover we are Americans!

Eating dinner at an outdoor café in Paris, we sat so close to the couple next to us it felt like we were dining together. We talked in hushed tones to respect the closeness. Seated on Hudson's right was a young man who leaned in and said he could hear us speaking English and wondered where we were from. He looked at his female companion in stunned surprise after hearing, "the U.S." Maintaining the hushed tone, Hudson offered some levity, "We're not all fat and loud."

Who am I and why am I here? I am not alone in asking myself these life questions. However, "What are you?" is a question we ask each other with surprising frequency in America. As if we are a breed of dog.

As a fourth-generation American, my shallow ancestry is a mix of western European countries. Travels with my son sparked a deeper curiosity about my core ancestry before the 1600s. Where did my ancestors from Western Europe originate and where did their ancestors come from?

Who was I?

A research project through National Geographic revealed my deeper ancestry. My DNA traces back to Sudan, in Africa. The genome project showed the migration path of my ancient ancestors, my deep heritage. It changed the way I looked at the world. Every time I met someone, I wondered if we were related. The differences were on the surface; I sought to uncover our similarities.

Traveling the world with my son brought me home. Home to who I really am and what I'm here to do. I reevaluated my values, my thoughts on the American dream, and the way I spend time and money.

I am a modern American woman and mother, a lifelong learner, and a citizen of the world.

Chapter 1

My Mother, Milk Bones, and Marriage

Be pithy.

That would be my two-word advice to my younger self. I imagine I have Miss Ryer, my fifth grade teacher at Huckleberry Hill Elementary School, to thank for this insight.

We moved from Brewster, New York, 20 miles east to Brookfield, Connecticut in July of 1972. I was 10 years old and excited to live in a house with an upstairs. Colonial-style wallpaper was popular then, and the dining room and my bedroom walls were covered in white, green, and gold harvest scenes and Revolutionary soldiers carrying flags.

Mounted over the front door, a shiny gold eagle with wings fully expanded proudly welcomed us.

"That will be the first thing to go," I heard my mom say.

She was angry.

She was born and raised in Yonkers, New York, just outside the city, and she had disdain for Connecticut. The eagle was a symbol not of freedom, power or victory, but of everything wrong with

Connecticut life. For her, the state was colonial, traditional, homogenized, white, pinched and uptight. She wasn't a cookie-cutter kind of woman and she didn't want to live a cookie-cutter kind of life.

Connecticut was not New York.

She prided herself on her heritage, and when she was mad, which was often, she would hiss through gritted teeth at me and my two younger brothers with a New York accent.

"Who do you think you are?" she would ask me, slowly emphasizing every single word. Before I learned what rhetorical meant, I would attempt a reply. "I just wanted to…" and was cut off by her glare. "Who asked you?"

It's funny to me now. But to laugh then meant exile to my colonial wallpapered room for an indeterminate amount of time. Years later, I would find myself in the interior design industry with a distinct distaste for wallpaper. When I came home with my fifth grade report card, there was no escape from her anger.

She was seated in her spot, in the corner seat of the family room sofa. Smoking a Kool cigarette and reading the newspaper. The family room was shades of dark brown with dark paneled walls. She hated paneling, especially Connecticut paneling.

I handed her my report card and stood in front of her as she pulled it out of the envelope. It showed ten grades handwritten in blue ink. It was my first year in Connecticut schools, and she had made more than a few comments about the New York schools being better.

Her brown eyes moved from the right side of the page to the left.

"Go get the dictionary," she said, without looking at me. For some reason, the dictionary was kept in the dining room hutch with the Thanksgiving plates.

I returned with the hard-bound burgundy book and handed it to her.

"Why do you need the dictionary?"

Ignoring me, she said, "Look up the word loquacious… l-o-q-u-a-c-i-o-u-s," she said, spelling it slowly.

I wanted to ask why, but kept quiet and flipped the book open, looking for the half-moon indentation for the letter L. I separated the pages searching for the word loquacious.

"Here it is," I said, hoping to make her happy.

"Read it," she said.

I ran my pointer finger across the page and said, "It means excessively talkative."

I looked at my mom's face for some hint of what this all meant.

She looked back at the report card and read the teacher's comments.

"Laura has continued to demonstrate a conscientious attitude toward her work. However ...."

She stopped reading to look me in the eyes.

Ok, I thought, this is where the dictionary comes in.

"However," she continued, "she has become a bit too loquacious at times."

I still didn't get it. In my mind, I was a good student. I offered a lot to the class, raised my hand all the time. I had a lot of good information to share.

"What did I get in conduct?" I asked.

"The lowest grade on this report card is your conduct grade," my mom said, without a smile. "B minus."

I was confused. B minus wasn't that bad.

"All your other grades are good," she said handing me the report card. I studied it, A's, B's, and a B plus in handwriting. There it was — the anchor, the B — and there was the word, loquacious, written in Miss Ryer's perfect cursive handwriting.

It's not a word I run into often, but when I do, I am brought back to that autumn afternoon in a paneled room filled with cigarette smoke in Brookfield, Connecticut.

By the time my mom died in 1990, at the age of 54, she had taught me many things about being a modern woman. I was 28, and through her unwavering belief in me, I felt capable of anything. She lived vicariously through me, her oldest of three children and only daughter. I was a woman with more choices than she had.

If your biography becomes your biology, then the site of mom's disease told all.

My mom's handwriting was remarkable. A surprise coming from her small, tense hands, with nails bitten down as low as you can before hitting blood. The thumbnail on her left, her writing hand, was permanently split. She'd slammed it in a taxicab door when she was a teenager. She wrote neatly and fluidly, her words clear and large. Her handwriting looked and felt confident and strong. She was the only one in the family who was left-handed. When she started writing sloppily, having a hard time controlling the pen, she went to a doctor. She was sent home in a neck brace.

"They think I have a pinched nerve," she told me, my two brothers, and dad.

For several weeks mom wore the brace, and her handwriting did not improve. When she returned the brace to the doctor, they scheduled her for an MRI. There was no pinched nerve. An inoperable, golf ball-sized tumor was embedded in her brain.

"I just want seven more years," she told us.

Instead of focusing on the diagnosis, I wondered why she wanted only seven more years. I didn't realize the clock was already ticking.

I looked at my dad, who seemed small all of a sudden. He just stood there, with his 300-pound body and slumped shoulders, and said nothing. Talking about feelings was not something we did well in my house.

I was not loquacious at home.

My mother didn't have seven years. She lived just short of one year. Her final words to me were, "everyone should have a daughter."

When mom died, I was in shock. I had been convinced that she would beat it. I believed she was stronger than cancer. After all, she was my mother, and we still had things to do together, a lot of things. We had places to see and there was still so much I needed to learn from her. It was 1990 and I was living in Manhattan, the city she taught me to love. I hoped to share it with her as I moved there, buoyed by her encouragement.

When I think of my mom, I feel her hand at my back, and hear her say the word "go" in my ear. I know that I can do whatever I set my mind to do. She instilled confidence in me, a belief that with effort and hard work I could do anything.

To be true to our story, it wasn't always this way. I was strong-willed, and we had our differences. The summer between high school and college was filled with three months of silence. I don't remember what happened, but I'm sure it had to do with something mouthy I had said. Perhaps it was another episode of teen-age angst, an indicator that it was time for me to leave the nest.

My first semester in college, I came home for Thanksgiving.

"What are you planning to major in?" she asked.

"I'm thinking about English and Philosophy. Maybe a double major."

Considering my answer, she looked at me, her brown eyes locking my own.

"English and Philosophy," she repeated, mulling.

I nodded.

Without blinking, she hit me between the eyes. Deadpan, she said, "And what will you do with that, sit on a barstool and bullshit for a living?"

It was rhetorical, and I knew better than to offer anything in reply. Instead I sat holding her gaze, waiting for her to tell me what I would major in.

"English and Journalism," she answered, without a question. "Then you can get a job."

When I graduated four years later, with a BA in English and Journalism, my focus was on writing for a newspaper. My studies emphasized objectivity, the neutral middle ground. A long way from the journalism of today.

I moved to Atlanta, Georgia, to write for a small rural weekly newspaper. But I'd been raised in the northeast, and the culture shock of rural Georgia never eased for me. And 18 months later when I left, ultimately, it was because of my lack of objectivity.

My editor had asked me to meet with a man representing the Ku Klux Klan. Up until that point I had been given very soft, fluff pieces. I wrote about a nearby nudist colony, a woman who suffered from endometriosis, and local small-town politics.

I remember questioning Chuck, the soft-spoken editor: "Really? The KKK still exists?"

It was during that meeting that I learned the power of public relations. PR is fueled by press releases, and there is always a who behind every story. In this case, it was a tall clean-cut man with a well-organized and neatly outlined KKK agenda. It included a meeting, a march, and a speech given by David Duke, the Grand Wizard of the KKK.

Such was the culture in all-white Forsyth County at the time. A PR visit from a representative of the KKK was a normal thing.

I attended the meetings and the march and listened to David Duke's rhetoric of hate, and I understood two things:

First, that a good-looking passionate speaker can win over a crowd even if they don't understand all of his words. Immediately, I understood how Hitler came to power and won over all those Germans. Second, I needed to find another job.

I could not use my writing to promote hatred and ignorance, and that was what I was being asked to do. So much for objectivity: I had an opinion and couldn't pretend otherwise.

I felt afraid. Now what? I had felt so clear about my life goal; now it did not work for me.

"You are having an existential crisis," a friend said.

"What the hell does that mean? And how do I fix it?" I snapped back.

I was being directed down another path.

I picked up a copy of *What Color is Your Parachute?* by Richard Nelson Bolles. I read it and did all the exercises. I identified my passions and skills to discover other fields where they could be used.

Journalism and sales may seem like a complete departure from each other. However, they are more similar than different. What I loved about being a journalist (hearing the stories, meeting new people, hitting deadlines, the autonomous schedule, and creating something from nothing) — also applied to sales. Except it was easier, and the pay was better. Both career choices were about connection and communication.

I left Atlanta and my dream of being a writer. I returned to the northeast to start what would become a 25-year career in sales. I felt muddled at this point of my life. A vague feeling of disappointment in myself for not "cutting it" as a journalist and perhaps for selling out and going into a career that was not what I went to college for. I was happy to leave Georgia, though.

While I was on my path to figuring out Who I Was, I also needed to be clear about Who I Was Not. One thing was clear: I was not a steel magnolia.

A series of connections from my father landed me a sales position with Nabisco. I went from thinking and writing about white supremacy à la David Duke to talking about the features and benefits of mint-flavored Milk Bones, aka dog biscuits. It would seem my life purpose was more than exposing southern racism. How could I be concerned with that when there was bad dog breath out there? I was going to be part of the solution.

It was the beginning of what I have come to understand as the "golden handcuffs" of the corporate world. This included a salary and bonus, a company car, sales meetings at nice hotels in interesting cities and paid tuition at the University of New Haven, as I started an MBA in Marketing.

This was a large, well-known corporation, cushy and secure. All I had to do was summon some enthusiasm for bad dog breath, or at least act like I cared! Easy. My words would now be used to benefit a corporation and me, and not used in a humanitarian way, as I had visualized in college.

It was around this time I heard the phrase "drinking the Kool

Aid." I understood that meant believing the core values of the corporation: to sell and make profits. There was a palpable complacency there, a comfort and an attitude of what more could you want? All your needs are taken care of. When I look back now, all I see is narcissism. Theirs and mine.

Selling mint-flavored Milk Bones was the start to my sales voice. There was an audience (as it turned out, lots of people didn't like the way their dogs' breath smelled) and I was there to help. I had purpose, a mighty clean-smelling purpose. Perhaps this was how I could change the world, one dog at a time.

At least I wasn't sitting on a barstool, bullshitting.

Two years later I got a phone call and left the mint-flavored Milk Bone world. A college friend contacted me about a sales position in her company, a different industry. She said, "It's selling leather to architects and interior designers. The territory is Manhattan." I'd found the words for dog biscuits; surely I would find them for leather.

Learning a new industry (interior design) and a new product (Italian upholstery leather), was not as compelling to me as moving into the city. I had grown up 90 minutes north of New York and went into the city often. My mom, with rolls of quarters in her purse for bus fare, would take me to watch the gay Halloween parade rain or shine, go to the Frick Museum, or just walk around.

My mother loved the city. She openly enjoyed seeing people letting their freak flags fly. The crazier, the better. A day in New York was the perfect antidote to Brookfield, Connecticut.

Nabisco was a comfortable job with a company car and autonomy. They were a secure, known company and they were willing to pay for my MBA.

I needed guidance. I called my parents for insights on this new offer. They each gave me different advice.

My father took me to lunch in West Haven, Connecticut and for three hours told me why he thought it was a bad idea to move into the city. Why leave a safe, secure and known company and job? He worked for Nabisco at the time, and I think he liked having me know his world.

Until this point in my life, I was a father's daughter. Making my dad happy was my goal. I played a lot of sports, including softball, which he'd also played when he was younger. I would mow the lawn and clean the yard and house, all with the purpose of his approval.

The three-hour lunch taught me something about myself and my dad. He advised me to stay because it suited him; he was not thinking of what would be the best choice for me. I was a girl and he was a chauvinist. "Oh shit, it's a girl," is what he said when I was born. I had been disappointing him since my arrival.

On the phone, my mom snapped her opinion in one pithy sentence: "You're 27 and single, go to New York." There was no room for doubt with her advice, which I took, leaving the known and moving into the unknown.

Selling leather to designers awakened me to a new love, interior design. Meeting with designers and learning about their vision for a space was endlessly creative and dynamic. Although leather was a small part of the overall design plan, I had access to the entire creative interior process. The materials, textures, and colors were fascinating to me. I learned something new every single day.

During those early New York years, I grew as a person exponentially. Until that point, my life was contained and constrained. Being a sales rep in that exciting city helped me to develop confidence and curiosity. The combination of meeting new people and developing relationships while learning the city was a potent blend that exhilarated me daily. The city taught me how to take care of myself, make things happen, and figure it out.

It was during those early years that I learned about diversity, about other foods and cultures and, most importantly, other ways to think and to live. Manhattan sparked my desire to experience and learn. I was expanding. And then my mother died.

The last pictures I took of mom were on our back porch in Brookfield. It was July. She was wearing a wig and her face, without eyelashes and eyebrows, was round from chemo. A complete physical departure from the attractive, vivacious woman she had been, pre-cancer.

Before the diagnosis she was attractive in a movie star, glamorous kind of way. She wore heavily lidded eyes and lipstick. She always looked put together. When I was young she wore a fire engine-red scarf on her head and smoked cigarettes. Even the way she smoked looked sophisticated. She would draw on a Kool and extend the smoking hand slightly behind her. It all looked sexy to my elementary-school-age eyes.

She reluctantly agreed to let me take her picture on the porch that hot afternoon. She hated the way she looked. I assured her that next year at this time we would look back at these pictures and see how far she had progressed.

She died two months later.

I was ten months into my new job, new industry, new city and new life. I channeled all the grief and sadness into work. A one-dimensional workaholic, I spent many days in angry disbelief. I directed all my choked-up emotion into selling leather for interiors. If I could talk about surface materials and concerns — stay on the top layer, the veneer — then I could avoid talking about what was going on in my interior. I was in this diminished, emotionally needy state when I met my future husband.

Wick and I met at an industry party. He worked in operations at the factory in Pennsylvania. I took a lateral move from leather to textiles, leaving sales for an opportunity to learn marketing.

"You never get a second chance to make a first impression" was my motto that night. I used all my sales muscle to get to know the new group of people I would be working with.

Wick and I were introduced; it wasn't love at first sight. We talked about textiles and the company. He told me he was married with two children. He was living in Allentown and had an excellent reputation within the company. I was living in a condo on West 14th Street, my first real estate purchase.

Wick's voice was different. Later I would tell him he had a voice made for radio, smooth and charismatic. He made even the most banal subjects sound exciting. I enjoyed talking with him. He was enthusiastic and offered to help with my textiles learning curve. His entire career was textiles and he was knowledgeable.

There's a poem, written by an unknown author, which suggests we meet people for a reason, a season, or a lifetime. I met Wick for many reasons. He has been one of my best teachers.

He was emotional and outspoken, and could sing like Frank Sinatra. He was funny and goofy and very intelligent, and I liked him. We talked a lot on the phone about the business of textiles. He taught me about the technical aspects, talking in his radio voice.

To this point in my life, I had dated a certain type of man, and Wick wasn't it. We weren't opposites, so that cliché did not apply. Married men and men I work with were not part of my history. Until I met Wick.

We broke the rules, we made mistakes, we laughed a lot, we talked about textiles, and we started a romance. He would come up to Manhattan for meetings and we would go out for a drink afterwards. He filed for a divorce and moved into my apartment. I was doing a lot of things for the first time, and it felt novel and exciting.

At the time I didn't realize it, but he was helping me heal from the death of my mom. That untended, unacknowledged pain sat calcified in my gut. I talked, cried, and talked and cried, with Wick about my mom. I let the feelings out, and I felt them all.

I married him, becoming his fourth wife. I thought I had some magic the earlier women did not.

I was different for Wick, too. I was strong, independent, and financially secure. He promptly put me on a pedestal, and I let him. I liked it. It felt good to be adored and admired even though it was artificial and lacked intimacy.

We both adopted a marriage and life of show. We became good actors together. Our focus was on the exterior, giving a good image and impression.

In hindsight, it should have been a short affair for both of us.

Turns out I had some anti-divorce beliefs I didn't know I had. Plus I was very attached to his son and daughter.

Now I understand all the marriage jokes, I thought.

When do you know when to walk away or try harder?

What was good for ten minutes lasted 10 years.

I stayed too long.

The good news: I healed from the grief of my mother's death. The best news: I had a son.

Until I gave birth to Hudson on September 8, 1999, every day of my pregnancy I craved one food: watermelon. Perhaps this was a bit of foreshadowing, because when Hudson was born he weighed nine pounds five ounces, about the same as the average watermelon. (The average American baby weighs seven pounds seven ounces.) When I held him it was like holding a watermelon, which filled me with surprising confidence, as he wasn't as small and fragile as I had imagined.

The pregnancy and birth were indicators of the type of child Hudson would be. He was an easy baby, alert and curious. We could and did take him everywhere. He went to London with me twice while I was pregnant. Even then I knew he was fun and easy to travel with.

By the time Hudson was born, Wick and I had moved out of the city up to Westchester County. His daughter Adrianna was eleven and his son John was eight. We spent every other weekend with them, and I attribute my deeper understanding of motherhood to them. Like Wick, John and Adrianna were great teachers. Until they came into my life in 1993, I had not spent a lot of time with kids. They taught me what kids need. I am a more confident mother because of the years I spent with them.

My marriage was not working and it wasn't healthy. Wick was having an affair with a woman in the warehouse. I knew it, and with a firm belief in sticking it out, anti-divorce style, I saw no way out. I thought marriage was forever. I was stuck. I lived in emotional fear and pretense.

When I reflect back on those days, I realize how little I trusted my intuition. I believed Wick's words over my feelings. My denial of my unhappiness and feeling of lack of choice, combined with Wick's affair, created an anxious, uptight, and narcissistic me. I became an actress. I pretended to be happy.

I wanted things to be a certain way. I wanted perfection. I denied my truth for the perceived security of a bad marriage. I sacrificed personal integrity for perceived security. I had two panic attacks and developed a pre-cancerous polyp in my colon. The doctor said, "if you had waited any longer, we would be having a different conversation."

I got help and guidance from a counselor. "I stayed too long" became my sound bite when people asked what happened to our marriage. I thought I was unique in staying too long. I am not unique at all. People have been staying too long in relationships long before my marriage ended. People stay too long in jobs and careers and geography and in physical places, too.

Staying too long is an attitude, rooted in fear and a belief that security is more important than integrity.

Here's what happened when I told myself the truth. I started to relax, breathe deeply, stay calm, and listen — and hear — better. I went to the gym, reconnected with old friends, worked on getting myself back. I took a year off from men. My intent was to get myself back, as I had given some of myself away in those thirteen years.

Hudson was seven years old when we got divorced. Telling him was the most difficult thing I have ever done.

"I thought I was going to have a good life," was the first thing Hudson said.

"You said you were never getting divorced," was the second.

Hudson and I talked a lot about what life would look like after the divorce. I told him he had two parents who love him and will love him no matter what happened. It was a tender and honest time. Though I knew it hurt Hudson, I also knew the bigger lesson was about honesty. Staying in a marriage for the kids is a sham. The kids can feel the fakeness and lack of intimacy.

I felt sad for hurting my son, guilty about making his life harder, angry at myself for lying to myself for so long, ashamed that I had settled and thought so little of myself. I was afraid of the unknown future, wounded because I don't fail well, and alone in the knowledge that I had wanted things to be a certain way and they weren't.

But I also felt a deep sense of knowing. I knew Hudson would be all right and so would I. I felt relief. The pretending was over, and with the constraints of marriage off me, I felt like I could breathe again. I felt true to myself; I felt clear. I felt the nervous excitement of not knowing what the future would bring. I could see my imperfections and didn't try to hide them. I allowed myself to feel everything and cried a lot.

But the most important feeling was that of honesty. I was being true to myself and my needs. My people-pleasing days were behind me. Don't do that again, Laura, I would tell myself.

I always want to change. I want to keep evolving. That is one reason I won't get a tattoo. What I think is funny or wise today may not apply in a decade. If I were to get a tattoo, though, it would be: Fear Less, Live More. Or maybe Expect Less, Learn More.

I stayed too long.

For more than a decade of my life, I stayed too long, listening to the outside world, not the inside voice. This is the story of how I got my voice back.

CHAPTER 2

Building Confidence

By the time Hudson arrived via C-section on September 8, 1999, he was already a frequent flier.

Two trips to London, daily commutes in and out of NYC to SoHo to cover Manhattan via the subway, bus, taxi and foot. When I was two months pregnant, we spent Valentine's Day weekend at a Vermont inn with another couple, and a few months later attended an annual sales meeting in Telluride, Colorado. While doing a presentation on color trends, I found myself gulping for air as pregnancy and high altitude challenged my thirty-seven year-old lungs. We even made a few road trips to Kennebunkport, Maine, to visit family.

He was an easy baby and an avid learner from infancy. Three months after he was born, we took our first major outing, to the Bronx Zoo. It was a balmy December day and I forgot to bring a pacifier. Hudson remained calm and occasionally napped. Looking at him in the stroller, so peaceful, gave me a feeling of confidence. I can do this, I thought to myself.

With each outing, I became calmer and more capable, and my confidence as a new mother grew. We added day trips to NYC and weekends in Maine. When he was nine months old, his first flight was to Disney World with John and Adrianna. And when he was a month shy of his fourth birthday, we rented a house in Impruneta, Italy, south of Florence, with friends from London. Closer-to-home trips included Bermuda, Pennsylvania, New Jersey, Massachusetts and Connecticut.

In 2001, we left New York and moved up to the Connecticut shoreline. Both Boston and New York City were easily accessible, and in 2006 Hudson and I took Amtrak up to Boston. I was still married then, and this was my first trip alone with my son for an extended time. Hudson was six years old and in first grade.

I can understand why some parents elect to stay home and not travel with kids. It's easier to stay home. But one of my goals as a mother is not to do things the easy way. The best things in life are often the hardest, and traveling with kids is both rewarding and exhausting. It is rigorous — experiencing new places, sites, foods and modes of transportation requires awareness and stamina.

What is most important to me is exposure to other ways of living and doing things. I am not just raising a son; I am raising a citizen of the world. I am exposing him to different people, with lives and cultures that may offer a contrast to our own, as my goal for my son is open-mindedness, compassion, and a worldview.

So in February 2006, we drove to New Haven's Union Station and purchased roundtrip Amtrak tickets to Boston's South Station. When we got to the Long Wharf Marriott hotel, a surprise was waiting in our room.

My cousin Barbara had worked in the hospitality industry and had arranged a little something extra for us upon arrival. We checked in and took our luggage and room key to the elevator. Hudson was excited about going to the New England Aquarium to see and touch the sting rays. Our fifth floor room looked out over the Boston Harbor.

Then we saw them. On the desktop, a large white plate full of warm chocolate chip cookies with a welcome note from Barbara and wishes for a fun weekend. She had worked for Marriott for 17 years. She knew the cookies would delight us, and she was right.

Hudson immediately ate three cookies, and then said, "I want to touch a sting ray."

Our plan the following morning was to meander, find the Freedom Trail and walk it. It was bitter cold, and after a short time outside we elected to get on a shuttle bus, the get-on, get-off type where you can get on to thaw out and get off to explore. We ended at Faneuil Hall, built in 1742, an urban marketplace once the site of famous speeches encouraging independence from Britain. Faneuil Hall, Quincy Market and North and South Markets all sit on a cobblestone promenade with shops and food.

Mentally and physically tired, we headed back to the hotel. Back in the room, I relaxed while Hudson jumped on the beds and watched SpongeBob on TV.

The next morning after check-out we wheeled our suitcase back to South Station to catch the Amtrak train home to Connecticut.

I had done it. My first solo trip with my son! No problems or issues. My confidence in traveling with my son solo was growing. For a while after that trip, Hudson thought hotel rooms came with a plate of chocolate chip cookies.

My love of New York City has never diminished. Just as my mother sparked a passion for the city in me, I wanted to do the same with Hudson. I have learned about the value of spontaneity and flexibility since becoming a mother and apply those when we go into the city. We live a few miles east of New Haven, CT and the Metro-North trains run regularly to Grand Central. Our trips into the city are relaxed and because we go in so often, we don't pack in too much in a visit. We prefer quality over quantity.

What do our children remember? What do we remember? I thought about what Hudson would remember as we headed to the Central Park Zoo. Hudson loved the zoo because it features, among other things, polar bears.

When I recall walking in New York with my mom, I remember how her energy changed. Walking through Grand Central, she transformed into a New Yorker. Chewing gum, she walked faster and talked to me often over her shoulder as she was one step ahead of me, so anxious was she just to be there.

Although its proximity to Grand Central is a 15-minute walk, that's not the only reason Hudson and I often go to the U.N. We have toured the inside and bought world flags in the shop. We have observed protesters picketing outside, causing us to go home and research the issue of the day. We have come to understand the world in a different way by reading the signs of the protesters. One of my favorite pictures of the U.N. is of Hudson standing next to the knotted gun sculpture Luxembourg gave the U.S.A. as a gift of peace.

"We just visited 193 countries," Hudson once said when we left the U.N.

My sojourns with my son are preparing me for bigger and more diverse trips in the future. The ability to travel as a single parent is important to me. Travel, adventure and learning are passions of mine, passions that have withstood my personal changes and evolutions. Perhaps the most vulnerable thing about me is my son. I can endure anything, but when I travel with Hudson I am exposed.

Mothers are quick to talk about how much they love their children and that they would and could do anything, sacrifice anything for them. Although I know the source of my strength is from my scar tissue, I don't want my son to have to suffer for his wisdom. Taking him out into the world forces me to trust the world and its people, and to know that we will both be safe and wiser for the journey.

A piece of unsolicited advice to mothers: Don't be completely selfless in raising your kids. Maintain your core person and share your interests and passions with them. This way they don't grow up believing they are the center of the universe and you will sustain your role as mother and not become a martyr.

Our next adventure was to Washington, DC over a frosty Veterans Day weekend 2007. We traveled on Amtrak, as it is easy, affordable and far less stressful than driving. When asked about his memories of that weekend, Hudson says, "I remember Rick the fish."

The Kimpton Hotel Monaco on 700 F Street NW in Washington, DC must have someone in marketing who understands children. It was the usual check-in, with one minor deviation. When the front desk personnel were done taking my credit card information they focused their attention on Hudson. They knew his name, as that was part of the check-in protocol.

"Hi Hudson, welcome to the Monaco Hotel," the friendly young man at the front desk said as he walked around from behind the desk to face Hudson.

Hudson said, "Hi."

"Would you like a goldfish for your room while you are here?" he offered.

Hudson looked up at me, I nodded, and he replied, "yes."

"Okay, you get yourselves settled into your room and your goldfish will be there momentarily," the employee promised.

Feeling like this trip was off to a great start, we walked through the highly stylized lobby down the hall to our room, which was decorated with mod wallpaper and very colorful upholsteries. Within moments of entering the room, there was a knock at the door.

"Who is it?" I asked.

"Room service. We have your fish," came the reply from the other side of the door.

I opened the door. A young man entered carrying a glass bowl with a goldfish. He placed it on the windowsill and set a card next to the bowl.

The card read: "Hi, my name is Rick."

"Mom, his name is Rick," said Hudson reading from the card. He was thrilled and looked into the bowl, watching Rick swim around.

The International Spy Museum, walking distance from the hotel, was our first destination. Hudson, reluctant to leave Rick, assured his new friend that we would be back soon. With timed entries into the museum, we bought tickets and entered within 15 minutes.

Touted as an interactive museum for all ages, it did not disappoint. As we walked through exhibits of everyday items highlighting the clever transformation of shoes, umbrellas, watches, pipes, lipstick containers, and pens into gadgets, we heard thumping and muffled voices overhead.

"Where is that noise coming from?" Hudson asked me. I heard it too, and found an employee to ask.

"There's a duct system overhead that is part of the spy experience," the man explained. "You can enter it over there," he finished, pointing to a well-concealed door in the corner of an exhibit.

"Can we both go in it?" I asked.

"Yes, but you will be on your hands and knees, crawling through ductwork," he said. "There are some peepholes to look through and you can see people below." .

Hudson wanted to go and I didn't. Fair enough. He was eight and I was forty-six years old. He was completely focused on the rustlings overhead. I hesitated, thinking about him in there without me, and finally trusted he would be ok.

He was. He crawled through the extended ductwork and talked to me through the ceiling. I couldn't see him but he could see me. We met at the end of the exhibit and he emerged happy and safe.

It is moments like this that I have needed to learn to trust the world and my kid. Passing along fear and skepticism will only breed a fearful, timid person. Trust and a little bit of letting go will cultivate confidence in Hudson. Control and fear will not. We have enough control and fear in the world. If I have faith in him, he will have faith in himself. A constant push me-pull you tension, parenting is.

Offering a global perspective, the museum exhibit included black and white photos of spy aliases from around the world. Stories of espionage and lies once concealed, now revealed. We learned about the OSS (the Office of Strategic Services), the original United States intelligence agency formed during World War II. The OSS was active for two years and is the predecessor of the Central Intelligence Agency. Julia Child's biography was featured as part of the OSS story. Prior to her fame as a French chef, she was a spy.

We exhausted the museum and it us, but walking back to the

hotel, Hudson's mind was on the goldfish. "I wonder how Rick is," he said.

Kudos to this hotel for getting it right with kids: When we entered the lobby, the same tall, thin young man who had originally asked Hudson if wanted a fish in his room came right over to us.

"How is your day, Hudson?" he asked.

"Good," said Hudson.

"Are you having fun?" the employee asked.

"Yes," said Hudson.

"Are you heading back to your room?"

The employee was onto something.

We both nodded.

"Would you like some fresh just-baked chocolate chip cookies brought to your room?" he asked, smiling.

"Yes," both Hudson and I answered.

"We'll bring them right down."

The fish and the cookies were a good reminder to slow down. Pause. My inclination was to keep going. We were only there for two and a half days, and there was a lot to see and learn. Another reminder that faster is not better.

Traveling with a child is not fast or efficient. It is steady and deliberate and full of experiences that depart from the itinerary.

Since he could walk, Hudson has found treasures. On the sidewalk, in the grass, on the beach — trinkets, rocks, bits of broken jewelry. They all come home with us. He puts them on his desk as a display of found things. He sees hearts or love everywhere.

"That cloud is in the shape of a heart, the rock looks like a heart, my hot chocolate has a pattern in it and it looks like a heart," he would enthusiastically announce.

The following morning we woke up to a rainy cold Washington day. We took a cab over to the see the monuments. We walked right up to the seated Abraham Lincoln in the Lincoln Memorial and waited in line to enter the Washington Monument.

Hudson wore his navy blue winter coat with the hood up and

thick black gloves. He stood in front of the World War II Memorial for a photo. He was intrepid as we made our way to the Vietnam War Memorial, where we watched veterans hug and cry and touch the wall with the names of soldiers who had died. From there we walked to the Thomas Jefferson Memorial. Cold and tired, we finished at the FDR Memorial.

"Can we go back and see how Rick is doing, mom?" Hudson asked.

We took a taxi back and visited our goldfish. A few hours later, dry and rested, we ventured back out to go on a staff-led tour of the U.S. Capitol. At the end of the tour, the guide showed us to Rosa DeLauro's office, the U.S. Representative for the third district in Connecticut. She came out of her office, introduced herself to Hudson and asked him his name.

"Are you from Connecticut?" she asked him.

"Yes," he said.

"Where in Connecticut are you from?"

"Branford," he said.

"I live in New Haven, close to Branford," she offered.

Our U.S. Representative tried, but talking with a child can be one-sided. She interviewed him and he answered. I was struck by how accessible and friendly she was.

Rosa DeLauro is a petite woman with short brown hair and eyes and an ardent nature. She is attentive and wiry and fully present. It was my first time meeting her as well, and she didn't rush us out of the grey-and-white office. Thanking her and saying goodbye, we shook hands and walked out of the office.

I looked at Hudson and said, "Rick?"

He nodded, adding, "And cookies."

As we packed the next morning, Hudson said, "Mom, can Rick come home with us?"

"No, he belongs to the hotel and needs to stay here," I said.

I looked over and Hudson's eyes welled up.

"Can't we offer to buy him and bring him with us on the train?"

he suggested.

I stopped packing. Looking at Hudson, I felt his attachment to the fish. I had a flashback to when I was eight years old and we had a pet turtle.

I imagined us plodding through Union Station, getting on Amtrak after wheeling the suitcase, holding Hudson's hand and maneuvering a water-filled sandwich baggie with Rick sloshing around.

"We can't do it, Hudson," I said. "I know you've enjoyed your time with Rick, but we can't take him with us," I said.

He accepted my answer, blinking hard a few times.

On the Amtrak ride home, Hudson picked a window seat with a large white table. He created a game involving cards and marbles, outlined the rules and swiftly beat me at every hand. He loved the idea of eating on the train. After losing another hand, we walked up the train to the bar car for hot chocolates and a bag of pretzels.

Here's what I noticed about myself. When I am in a foreign or unknown setting, I rely on my intuition more. I feel and sense instead of think and analyze. This serves to release any fear, known or unknown. The feeling of being fearful evaporated once I honed my intuition. I honed it by slowing down and allowing myself to take in a place. What I once would have identified as fear I renamed excitement.

The train pulled into Union Station in New Haven. We disembarked and walked to the parking garage to find our car. We drove home in comfortable silence, wiser and weary from our trip.

Returning home from school one afternoon, Hudson told me they were learning about the Egyptians. And did I know they invented paper and pens?

Hudson is an avid learner and an excellent student. I recall the comment his first grade teacher offered in a parent-teacher conference.

"Hudson knows a lot of things about a lot of things," she said.

Approaching the world with curiosity is a rich way to learn. I feel one of my duties as his mother is to keep the learning going outside of school as well. But it is not all about him, either. I also love to learn, and with that intent we planned a visit to the Metropolitan Museum of Art and the Temple of Dendur.

The Temple of Dendur on the first floor of the Met is an Egyptian temple made of sandstone built in 15 BC. Offered as a gift from Egypt to the U.S., the temple sits in its own wing surrounded by an interior moat.

Hudson asked if he could bring his friend Andrew. They had been classmates and friends since the second grade.

I told Hudson yes. Both Hudson and Andrew have brown hair and brown eyes. They could be brothers. I have always liked their friendship, as it is easy and equal. They laugh a lot when they are together, and it makes me feel good to hear them. So Hudson asked Andrew if he wanted to go to New York City with us for the day to see a real-life mummy.

Our plan set, we left Branford early Saturday morning for Union Station in New Haven to get on a Metro-North train to Grand Central. The three of us sat together, Hudson at the window, Andrew in the center and me on the aisle. They talked and laughed and pointed out the window as I read.

When we arrived in Grand Central, they both announced they were hungry. There are a lot of choices for food in the lower level of Grand Central. Hudson and I ate falafels while Andrew ate a slice of pepperoni pizza. Then we left Grand Central and took the bus uptown to the Met. On the sidewalk at the base of the entrance steps were several hot dog vendors.

"Can we get hot dogs?" Hudson asked.

I looked at him and then Andrew.

"You just ate at Grand Central. How can you be hungry again?" I asked.

They both sheepishly shrugged and smiled.

"Those hot dogs are so good. Please, Mom?" Hudson said, as Andrew stood by, offering unspoken support for his friend.

"Sure, let's go get you two hot dogs," I conceded, walking up to the truck.

Sitting on the steps of the Met, the two boys ate their second lunch as I people-watched.

Our intent was surgical — to see the Temple of Dendur and find the mummy. After purchasing entry tickets, we looked around for the entrance to the Egyptian wing.

Loudly, I heard, "Where are the dead bodies?" I turned and looked at Andrew, who was waiting for an answer.

"Andrew! You've heard of indoor and outdoor voices? There's a third category: Museum voice. Use it today," I suggested.

We made our way to the Egyptian wing and serpentined our way to a far corner to see the mummy. It was nestled in a creepy, quiet corner. Both boys were giddy when they found it. They hovered and commented on how small the mummy was, and then were done. We made our way through the exhibits to the temple of Dendur, stopping occasionally to study artifacts in a case or read descriptions of Egyptian culture and beliefs.

Surgical it was. We saw what we came to the museum to see and were ready to venture downtown to the 9/11 memorial. We walked to the subway entrance and headed downtown.

"What is our stop?" Hudson asked.

"42nd Street, Grand Central," I answered.

At 42nd Street we stepped off the train and walked across the platform with the plan to board the next #5 downtown. The platform was crowded and the boys and I waited. When the train arrived, there was a crush of people boarding and then the bing bing indicating the doors were closing.

We were not going to fit into that train. Hudson and I stepped back, but Andrew continued and boarded. The doors shut and I slammed my hands open-palmed onto the glass of the shut doors.

"Andrew!" I yelled, panicked. He stared back at me.

As I started to think what to tell him, the doors opened and the woman behind him pushed him off and the train pulled away. I mouthed "thank you" to her as the train left the station.

Andrew, stunned, leaned against the gritty white tiles of the subway platform.

"Andrew, what were you doing?" Hudson implored.

"Andrew, what would you have done if that train pulled away?" I asked, suddenly exhausted at the possibility of what if.

He slowly, silently slid down the wall into a crouch.

"I don't know," was all he said.

As the next #5 pulled into the station, I put my hand on Hudson and Andrew's back and we three entered the train and sat down. At Fulton Street we got off and climbed the stairs to street level and got our bearings. As we walked towards the 9/11 memorial, surrounded by tourists and make-shift memorials, Andrew yelled out, "Look at that!"

The immediate area around the site of the September 11, 2001 terrorist attacks was covered with notes, cards and photos pinned up on fences and billboards. A raw, tender authentic mood with quiet solemnity, set the tone for the neighborhood.

"It's a two-level Burger King!" he exclaimed.

His panic over the subway snafu behind him, Andrew was thrilled to see something he had never before seen in his life ... a double-decker Burger King.

"We're not eating again," I said, before being asked.

Andrew joined us another time on a different adventure in NYC at a museum across Central Park on the west side.

The American Museum of Natural History hosts a Night at the Museum every weekend, and for $129 per person it was cheaper than any decent hotel in the city. The accommodations were somewhat different than any hotel, as well.

Entering Central Park West and 81st Street carrying our sleeping bags, pillows and backpacks, we were directed to the check-in desk. They gave us packets of information and told us to take our sleeping bags and overnight gear and find a cot under the big blue whale. The museum was now open only to those who were spending the night.

We found three army-green Coleman cots together. The huge female blue whale replica weighs 21,000 pounds, and our cots seemed tiny under her massive belly. The cots, about eight inches off the ground, were snuggly positioned with just enough room to slide in.

"Where are the flashlights?" Hudson asked as he opened the backpack. "Found them. Here, Andrew."

Hudson said, "Mom, we're going to find the dinosaur exhibit."

I nodded and said, "I will meet you there."

One of the key attractions of Night at the Museum, aside from having the entire museum to ourselves, was the darkened hall in the Age of Dinosaur exhibit.

"I will find them," I thought. "I'll just follow the screams."

Even though we had visited the museum many times, it was even better during the Night at the Museum events. There were no crowds and we could access everything. We lingered on some of the exhibits with time to absorb and observe more thoughtfully.

The museum was ours until the following morning, lights out at midnight. I lay back on the Coleman cot surrounded by 400 friends I hadn't met yet. I added urban camping to our list of life adventures.

Every visit to New York is different, but they all end the same. We leave tired, smarter, happy and, always, with a Magnolia Bakery cupcake in our hands.

Since I'd confidently mastered the art of traveling solo with Hudson in the United States, I decided to venture outside the country in the fall of 2009. We flew to the Atlantis Paradise Island resort, just 179 miles south of Florida.

A steel drum band was playing in the Bahamian airport when we arrived. The music, combined with coral pink interior walls, set the mood for a first adventure outside our native country. We found our way through the packs of fellow tourists and were taken by shuttle to the resort.

The ride from the airport to the luxury resort was a journey of paradoxes. As we rode through the very poor streets of Paradise Island, we could see the Atlantis in the distance, like Oz on the horizon. Immaculately landscaped, the grounds were perfect and everywhere we looked was water — pools, slides, lagoons, and fish tanks.

Upon entry to the room, Hudson said, "I want to go swimming!"

Settled into the resort, we found a cabana and bought lunch. Each day as we maneuvered through lunches and dinners, the prices never ceased to amaze me. Jaw-dropping prices for everything, including a tuna wrap poolside.

After lunch we rode a two-person transparent tube down the lazy river, occasionally bumping into other drifters. The river featured surges of whitewater and spontaneous overhead showers. We were relaxed and excited. We wanted to swim with the dolphins and headed over to Dolphin Cay and signed up for a shallow-water interaction.

After signing release papers, we were given wetsuits and sent to an outdoor locker to wriggle into them. Walking to the edge of the pool, we saw dolphins swimming at the far end and were told many of the dolphins were rescued from Hurricane Katrina.

"The scars on the snouts and backs can be seen on some of the dolphins," the young woman trainer explained.

We were instructed to enter the pool and stood in belly-high water. The trainer blew a high-pitched whistle and a dolphin swam right over, stopping in front of us.

"You can touch the dolphin," she instructed, "just don't grab the dorsal fin or cover their eyes."

Hudson and I reached out to pet the dolphin. A photographer was snapping pictures from the edge of the pool.

"Look this way," said the photographer, then took our picture with the dolphin between us. The handler blew the whistle. The dolphin swished out into the middle of the pool and jumped in a high arch out of the water, creating a big splash and applause.

If we could swim with dolphins, why not sharks?

When you walk through Atlantis, there are fish tanks and replicas of ruins, opportunities to look through ceiling-high glass and observe all types of sea life. On the walk back from Dolphin Cay, we stopped often to look into lagoons and tanks and saw a ride that cut through the shark tank.

It took us a day to summon the courage to take on the serpent slide.

We climbed the steps to the top of the serpent slide and got into a transparent rubber tube. Shaped like the number eight, it was a tube built for two. We were both nervous taking off from the top of the corkscrew slide. The entry to the slide is dark, we sat in the tube with gushing water propelling and winding us for 30 seconds before we were plunked into the shark tank.

Sharks swam freely all around, as we were on display in the acrylic tunnel submerged in their tank. A subtle current slowly propelled us through the tunnel, giving us time to point out the hammerhead shark, a tiger shark and a bull shark. Eerily calm, they swam gracefully around us.

The serpent slide ended with a small dip into an exterior, shark-free pool.

We'd made it!

"Let's do it again!" Hudson said. "Come on, mom!"

He grabbed the handles of the inner tube and started back up the steps to the top to do it again. This time we were fearless. We swam with the sharks eight times that day.

Atlantis is a luxury resort and felt safe. It was a good first trip out of the country for us. Three days was the perfect amount of time to be there. We experienced the water slides, rides and lagoons and even went out to the beach and swam in the Atlantic one afternoon.

When we reflect back on that trip, we refer to Atlantis as the snow globe. It was protected, surreal, a departure from reality. Our travel acumen, confidence, and preferences were being shaped. We agree it was homogenized and antiseptic, and though we were happy to go, we would not repeat it. We were becoming discerning. Our appetite for the authentic was growing.

In December of 2010, I flew to Buffalo to attend a company Christmas party and brought Hudson with me. The party was three hours of our thirty-six hour stay.

Our time limited, we decided on two sites: The kazoo museum and Niagara Falls. Niagara Falls was obvious. But we'd recently discovered there was a kazoo museum, south of Buffalo. The website assured us that we would learn about the creation and story of the kazoo, the "most democratic of instruments."

But a lake-effect snowstorm blew through the Five Towns, south of the city, and our plans to visit the kazoo museum in Eden, NY were cancelled. So we headed north to Niagara Falls.

Light and steady snow flurries framed our day. We viewed the falls from the New York side, and when we needed a respite from the cold, we went inside and walked through the museum, where we watched a movie about the history of the falls. Among other things, we learned someone did go over the falls in a barrel. It was a woman celebrating her 63rd birthday. She went over the falls and survived. The story has staying power, as it happened in 1901.

Sipping hot chocolate, we stepped outside intending to walk over the Rainbow Bridge to Canada to see the falls from that vantage point. We were told the view was superior, and it was.

We opted to drive over. Visiting Niagara Falls on a snowy December Saturday afternoon was a solitary excursion. We crossed over the Rainbow Bridge into Canada easily.

"I got there first," Hudson said, his arm outstretched over the dashboard into Canadian airspace. Parking along the river, we plunked coins into the meter and walked towards the falls for more pictures. Permanently squinting, coat hoods up, every picture of us that day looks painful with the powerful backdrop of the misty and icy falls. We both wore chunky red mittens with a white Canadian maple leaf stitched on top.

"People will think we're Canadians with these mittens on," Hudson joked as we walked toward a restaurant for lunch and warmth.

"Yes, they will, until they hear our American accents," I replied.

After lunch, as we walked back along the river, the combination of snow flurries and spray mist from the falls kept us moist. The roar of the falls and power of the water dumping over its cliffs caused us to pause again and again.

Once in the car, we started back to the Rainbow Bridge.

"Good-bye, Canada," Hudson said, waving his floppy wet red mitten at the falls.

I slowed the car as we approached border crossing patrol. The small booth looked like a U.S. toll station. I lowered the window and looked over at the policeman, who asked where we were from.

"The U.S.," I said.

He looked into the car.

"Do you have identification?"

I nodded.

"Hudson, can you pull our passports out of my bag, please?"

Hudson produced two navy blue U.S. passports. The policeman slowly studied them.

"Who is in the car with you?" he asked me.

"This is my son," I answered.

Then he looked in the car and directed the next question to Hudson.

"Is this your mother?" his intense gaze focused on my son.

"Yes," Hudson replied.

I thought, is there a problem? Has there been an abduction and they are questioning everyone with a child? Hudson has his father's last name, and I'd kept my name when I married Wick. Was it the two different last names? My heart started to pound, as he was not handing back the IDs, but instead studying them and flipping through the passport pages. Finally satisfied, he passed the passports back into my sweaty hands. I thanked him, for what I am not sure. Letting me keep my son, allowing me back into the U.S.?

Rattled, I drove through bleak, downtown Niagara Falls, NY back to the hotel with my son, in silence.

CHAPTER 3

Connecticut Choices

Staying in the house was important to me when I got divorced. It represented stability and continuity for me and Hudson. When the divorce was complete in September of 2007, we crafted the agreement to include me buying the house.

I loved that house on Harbor Street. Built in 1824, it was the prior residence of a sea captain and had great bones and wide-board pumpkin-pine floors. I had laid my heavy hand all over that house, painting the walls and wide molding with Zen-like patience, including horizontal stripes in the upstairs hallway.

We had moved there four years earlier, and I felt it was a great home for Hudson to grow up in. The piece de resistance was, unquestionably, the kitchen.

The prior owners had added on to the original structure, creating a 24' x 24' room with four exposures. The kitchen was the heart of the house, and we were lucky enough to have room for a sofa and chair along with an eight-seat kitchen table. I had thought Hudson and I would be there for the long haul.

So I was surprised in December of 2009 when I was ready to sell it. I woke up that cold morning and knew it was time to sell. I talked to Hudson about it and he was understandably emotional and resistant to the idea.

"It's too much house for us," I explained to my then nine-year-old son. "And it takes a lot of time and money to maintain."

"I like this house," he said sadly.

"I do too, Hudson. We have had a lot of good times here and we have a lot of memories made here," I said, feeling sad, too.

"I don't want to move."

"I know you don't. This house is too big for just the two of us," I explained. "When I get home from work, I would rather spend time with you than mowing the lawn and weeding the garden. I'd prefer to spend the money I make doing fun things together, instead of home repairs and maintenance," I said softly and firmly.

He cried. I cried.

We agreed to each write a letter to the house thanking it for all the fun years and providing us with shelter. I still have those letters and cannot read them without feeling very emotional.

I hired a realtor. The house was listed the first week of January. I called or emailed everyone I knew to start the marketing process.

"They say burying a St. Joseph upside-down in front of the front door facing the street will help sell a house," a friend informed me. Who knew? Within the week, the same friend presented me with a five inch tall St. Joseph ready for upside-down burial.

When is the right time of day to bury a saint in your front yard? I asked myself, feeling self-conscious about what the neighbors would think seeing me with a shovel, digging a shallow grave in January in Connecticut.

Never doubting the power of burying St. Joseph, I decided the best time was not during the day, but at night. After Hudson went to sleep, I went outside and dug a small hole for my good luck charm. Turning soil in January was harder than I expected. St. Joseph went into a three-inch hole, not the six inches suggested on the side of the box.

In he went, upside down, facing the street about four feet from the front door step.

"Do your work, please," I silently prayed and slid back into the house, shovel in hand.

Whether it was St. Joseph or the charm and location of a sea captain's house or good timing (my realtor had advised to wait for the spring market), the house on Harbor Street sold in six days, full price, to a problem-free couple.

You don't realize how many vases you have until you start to pack up to move. I had more than thirty. Some were from birthday or anniversary deliveries and some from traveling to Italy, where the glass was too gorgeous to pass up. In any case, there they were — out of the cabinet and on the kitchen table. Amazing when they were all out together.

Hudson walked into the kitchen as I was holding, admiring and reminiscing about one Salviati vase in particular.

"What are you doing, Mom?" Hudson asked.

"Looking at these vases and figuring out what to do with them," I answered.

"Why are there so many?" he asked, seeing some for the first time himself.

"Some were gifts, but many I bought because I loved them," I answered, placing the vase back on the table.

And then he said something that changed me forever, and I have often re-quoted.

With wisdom beyond his years, he looked at me and said, "Mom, the stuff doesn't love you back."

He was right. I had spent a lot of time, money, and energy getting and maintaining the stuff. It was there in the kitchen, in January of 2010, that I shifted. From that moment on, I decided that my time, money, and energy would be better spent on experiences than things.

With a buyer on the hook, I set out to downsize, to buy a smaller house. Nothing worked out, and getting near to the closing date, I elected to go on Craigslist and find a rental. Hudson and I looked at a few, a humbling experience coming out of our well-loved home.

We had looked at a handful when we settled on a two-floor apartment in the center of town.

I'd made a little money from the quick and painless sale of the house, so I asked Hudson a question.

"Hudson, let's go on vacation," I said. "Like a real, good vacation. Where do you want to go?"

Without hesitation, he confidently said, "France. I want to go to France and I want to go to Normandy."

It was as if he was waiting for me to ask him that question. He answered that quickly and knowingly.

It was decided. France would be our first trans-Atlantic trip.

CHAPTER 4

France

A friend recommended a travel agent in Hamden, Connecticut. I called John Weinstein of Adler Travel and made an appointment.

"Please bring your son with you," he advised.

I liked him already.

Hudson and I met with John and told him we wanted to go to France and see Normandy, and were open to suggestions for other places to go and see. Working around Hudson's elementary school calendar, we elected to go at the end of June.

John suggested starting in Paris, visiting the capital for four days. From there we would rent a car and drive northwest to Normandy. His suggestions included a two-day sojourn to Mont St. Michel and two days in Rouen.

I felt confident working with John. There I was, a single mother with my son. I felt vulnerable, but I wanted to travel, and I wanted to feel safe. His itinerary, knowledge and wisdom about the hotels, getting around, renting a car and general French culture assured me that Hudson and I would have a memorable trip.

Before we left Connecticut, Hudson packed his wallet with $38.75 in it. Upon arrival at Charles de Gaulle airport, we picked up our suitcase and went to the currency exchange counter. Hudson dumped all his American dollars and coins into the concave tray and pushed it under the window towards the clerk. The man looked up and smiled and pushed back euro bills and coins. His smile and the kind look he gave my son made me feel happy and confident.

We checked into the Richmond Opera hotel in Paris. We were given a heavy skeleton key to our room. Hudson opened the door to the room, then pushed the wheeled suitcase aside and ran for the bathroom.

"Mom, how do you flush a toilet in France?" he asked.

I walked in to see there was no flush lever, just a faucet.

The word bidet was added to Hudson's vocabulary that day.

It seemed right that the first site we took ourselves to was the Eiffel Tower. It was cliché, but appropriate.

We had napped after Hudson examined the bidet, and were ready for an adventure. It was a very long and beautiful walk to the Eiffel Tower. Along the way we occasionally heard crowds cheering for the World Cup soccer game.

We queued up to go in the Eiffel Tower and decided we wanted to take the diagonal elevator up. Packed into the glass square elevator, with nothing to hold onto, we leaned against other people and they did the same. The claustrophobia was offset by the amazing view of Paris from the top of the tower.

Our first iconic tourist site in Paris visited, it was time to eat! Outdoor bistros and brasseries lined the streets. We chose a tiny restaurant with four tables outside. The waiter directed us to one of the tables. Soon after, a couple was seated at the table right next to ours. They were so close to us that it felt like we were dining together.

From within the restaurant a live band played. The music from the accordion was lively and festive.

The waiter strongly suggested the fish of the day and we both ordered it. While we waited for our dinner, we talked about what we wanted to see the next day. We decided on Notre-Dame and the Louvre.

"But only to see the Mona Lisa, mom," Hudson said.

Consciously, we lowered our voices. The couple next to us was very close. We were aware of how much louder we spoke in comparison to non-Americans.

"Excuse me," the man seated at the table right next to us, said.

Hudson and I both looked over at him.

"Yes," we said in unison.

"I am from Belgium and my wife is from Luxembourg. We can hear you speaking English, but can't tell where you are from," he queried.

"We are from the U.S.," I answered. "We are Americans."

"Americans!" he looked at his wife, shocked.

Hudson noticed his shock. Leaning in, he offered, "We're not all fat and loud."

The man threw his head back, guffawed and laughingly nodded as if to say, "That's exactly what I was thinking!"

The next morning we had petit dejeuner at the hotel and walked down Avenue de l'Opéra to Île de la Cité and Notre-Dame. We witnessed three scams along the way.

In the first, a tanned older woman approached us and held out a handwritten note that stated she was a Bosnian refugee. She held her hand out as we read the note. She needed money to get back home to her family.

In the second scam, another older woman came from nowhere and dropped a gold ring on the ground, then offered to sell it to us.

In the third, in the shadows of Notre-Dame, an old hunchbacked woman cloaked in black extended her hand for money; nearby stood a younger man with a watchful eye on her. The irony of a hunchback near the Notre-Dame was not lost on us.

Hudson instinctively knew they were not authentic and said, "They know we are tourists and hope we'll fall for it."

We didn't and walked on. I nodded and thought about all three scammers being women.

Inside the Notre-Dame, Hudson took a picture of the cobalt

blue, red and gold stained-glass window. Unbeknownst to us at the time, that image would become our 2010 Christmas card.

From Notre-Dame, we walked along the Seine. We crossed the river headed for the Louvre, with one objective: to see the Mona Lisa. There was a line just for her. When we were next to see her, we were stopped by a velvet rope. Mounted on a wall all to herself, Mona Lisa demurely smiled from twenty feet away. The painting, covered in glass, was much smaller than we expected and magnificently beautiful.

As we left the Louvre, we spotted a small carnival.

"Mom, can we go over there?" Hudson asked.

I thought about the carnivals at home — greasy, overpriced and seedy.

"We can walk over and see what it's like," I answered.

The Parisian carnival was a lot classier than anything I had been to in the U.S. It was set in a park. A graveled pedestrian walkway lead us into the small carnival. There were rides and food vendors and a grey climbing wall.

"Mom, can I try climbing the wall?" Hudson asked.

The wall had occasional footholds. Kids were harnessed and scaled to the top, about fifteen feet up from the ground.

"Sure, you can climb the wall," I answered, looking for a place to buy tickets. Tickets purchased, Hudson handed them to the attendant and got into a climbing harness. He successfully scaled the wall three times. His efforts were rewarded with a plastic pistol.

Pride and pistol in hand, Hudson spotted an ice cream vendor. Saying nothing, he looked at the ice cream and then me.

"Because we are on vacation, you can," I answered, and we walked to the ice cream stand.

It was hot. 33-34° Celsius (low 90s F) and the front of the ice cream vendor showed evidence of the drippings of previous customers.

Hudson approached the window, pointing to the image of a chocolate and vanilla swirl on a cone. He was promptly handed his treat. I held his newly won plastic pistol as he attempted to beat the sun's effects on his ice cream.

The sun won. The cone had a small hole in the bottom. Within moments, Hudson was covered with ice cream — his hands, wrists and up to his elbows onto his shirt and shorts. Even his shoes had drippings. His smile never left his face.

Dessert was followed by dinner. Hudson amazed me and the waiter when he ordered and devoured 12 escargots.

On our third day in Paris, with the heat unrelenting, we decided to go to a movie. Our primary motive was to sit in an air-conditioned space for a couple of hours. We told ourselves we would figure out the French.

We purchased our tickets to the movie A-Team. We entered the theater, sat down and realized it was not air-conditioned. The upside? The movie was in English with French subtitles. After the movie, we walked across the street to an Indian restaurant for dinner.

We had recharged our energy, and on day four in Paris we set out early to Invalides to see the tombs of Napoleon and Louis XIV. The museum atrium had marble reliefs on the wall and Hudson interpreted and deciphered them. We were surrounded by yellow Brazil jerseys as the World Cup continued and Brazil was favored to win (they didn't).

In the museum shop, I bought a book on Invalides and Hudson bought a Napoleonic era replica gun.

"Please stop shooting me," I asked him, after he had aimed it at me several times.

Walking distance from the Invalides, the Rodin Museum was our next stop. Hudson counted the many dogs we passed along the way.

The Thinker was the first thing we saw when we entered the museum grounds. Set on a pedestal in the jardin, the famous sculpture was surrounded by rose bushes. I leaned in to smell and there was no scent. Hudson did the same and nodded enthusiastically.

"It smells great," he said.

We learned Rodin was late to his talents. When we entered the room with The Kiss, we found a hushed crowd admiring the marble work. For a museum housing such amazing sculptures, the building itself was tired and run down.

Exiting the museum, Hudson took the entry sticker off his shirt and stuck it on a pole on the street, with hundreds of others Rodin museum stickers.

We stopped at a corner bistro across from the museum for Cokes and, much to Hudson's dismay, plat du fromages.

"The cheese here stinks," Hudson said, wrinkling his nose. "How can you eat it?"

I have a long-standing, ardent love affair with cheese and nothing he said would sway me. There were many things I was looking forward to learning, eating, and seeing in France. Eating, specifically eating French cheese, was at the top.

The presentation of the cheeses was modest. I didn't catch all the descriptions of the various types presented, but it really didn't matter. I was planning on eating them all. As I ate, I thought if I ever open a restaurant in America, cheese as a dessert option would be on the menu. In the battle of chocolate vs cheese, cheese wins. All day. Every day.

After leaving the bistro, Hudson hailed his first French cab. He directed the driver to take us to the highest point in Paris: Montmartre, to the Sacré-Cœur Basilica.

We entered quietly. Mass was being said. Hudson walked to the candles, deposited some coins in the metal donation box and lit a candle. I felt very emotional in this church. I was thankful for the opportunity to be there with my son, and so thankful for so much goodness and abundance in my life. I wiped away tears as we walked out.

As we descended the steps, we saw a man making and selling pipe cleaner puppies. Surrounded by yellow Brazilian World Cup jerseys, we watched the man. He was seated in a wheelchair. He crafted the same puppy over and over in various colors.

Hudson picked a grey one with black ears. He picked out a

multi-colored one with white ears for me. We purchased them for 2€. Swinging our pipe cleaner puppies, we walked toward the crypt and paid 5€ to go into the dome of Sacré-Cœur.

The tight, spiraling staircase took us up an additional 260 feet. The winding claustrophobia-inducing stairs offered no sortie (exit) and was wide enough for one person. We leaned against the clammy walls as we ascended. The hellish walk up was rewarded by a panoramic view of Paris. Just outside the window were gargoyles. Their open mouths were gutters for water drainage. We saw Archangel Michael, with enormous wings, standing on what appeared to be an alligator.

The descent was faster, but deposited us in the creepy crypt with one sortie. We found it quickly and stepped outside to a loud clap of thunder and simultaneous lightning. The rain smelled wonderful. No one ran for cover. We all sat on the steps of Sacré-Cœur, sweat and rain mixed as the storm came and went.

I looked at Hudson seated next to me on the steps, and said, "Je t'aime."

Our last night in Paris was spent on the Ferris wheel, back at the carnival. A pinkish-red sunset and a night view of the Eiffel Tower were a poetic goodbye.

An observation: During this trip I became increasingly self-conscious about speaking only one language. Though I believe intuition is also a language, and I rely on my intuition heavily, it was here that I decided we both needed to learn another language.

There were times on this trip I felt arrogant for presuming people would speak English. When we returned to the U.S. I researched taking an adult French class. As for Hudson, he continued to take French in middle school and elected to start studying Russian outside school.

We woke up Saturday July 3, 2010 to rain. It was our day to depart Paris. We took a quick, quiet cab ride to Gare du Nord to pick up the rental car I had prepaid for back in the states. I opted for a smart car for its size and gas economy, but when we checked in at the very crowded rental counter, we were in for a surprise.

Remembering a line from Seinfeld, about taking a reservation but not keeping it, I started to sweat. How were we going to get to Bayeux?

"We can offer you a free upgrade," the car rental agent advised us. When I nodded, he slid a black key with a peace symbol on it.

I looked him in the eyes.

"A Mercedes?" I asked, incredulous.

"Will that be ok? It has no miles on it," he explained.

In hindsight we were lucky to have a bigger car as the drives to Bayeux, Mont St. Michel, and Rouen were long and aggressive. Driving a big, beefy car added to our confidence and comfort.

If only getting to the exterior peripheral were as easy. After a frustrating hour of driving around the Gare du Nord, Hudson with map in hand and patience waning, we spotted the street we needed to access the A13 west.

"Rue de la Chapelle. Mom. There!" Hudson said pointing to the street that had eluded us for the previous hour. My ten-year-old navigator and I breathed a loud sigh of relief.

An hour into the ride, we pulled over at a rest stop. Stretching our legs, we went inside and bought ham and cheese baguettes, drinks and peanut M+M's and a map of France.

Although driving a brand-new Mercedes station wagon was a surprise luxury, it lacked the one thing we needed — a GPS. Hudson plotted our A13 course west to Bayeux.

Five tolls later, each one more than the last, we exited and pulled over to ask directions to Chateau de Sully, our hotel.

The car had German license plates, and we were asked more than once on this journey where we were from. We both loved the anonymity.

"Wow!" Hudson said as we pulled into the long driveway that led up to the Chateau de Sully.

"You're not kidding, this is amazing," I said. Thank you John Weinstein for setting us up in style!

As elegant as it was, we quickly dropped our suitcases in room 15 and got back in the car and drove 5km to Omaha Beach.

The rural ride was untouched by any spectacle or reminder of June 6, 1944, and this surprised me. I had envisioned big signs pointing to the beaches and even a large hotel. Instead we passed rural farmland, timeless and beautiful, with long grass swaying and cows in the fields. Passing a few small rustic cafés and a church, we spotted a very small hand-painted sign with an even smaller arrow pointing toward an unpaved road that said "Omaha Beach."

It was clean, serene and peaceful. There were a few people on the beach throwing a Frisbee and others eating lunch. Hudson and I took our shoes off and walked along the edge of the water. We had read that occasionally shrapnel rolls up onto the beach. As we walked, we intently studied at the sand, but didn't see or find any.

One of my favorite photos from this trip was taken on this day. Hudson is squatting, looking into a small eddy on Omaha beach. The sun is shimmering off the water and the lighting is so subtle the picture looks like it was taken in black and white.

When I look at that picture of my young son, childlike and safe on the site of such a fierce, bloody battle, I feel that if I didn't already know what happened there, I would never guess. That is how peaceful it is.

We left the beach and drove to the cemetery, which was closed for the day. Back in the car, we stopped at one of the roadside cafés and ate croque monsieurs and frites and drank Oranginas. Our plan was to return the following day, July 4th, to the cemetery, museum and beaches.

We arrived at the 172-acre cemetery that is home to 9,387 graves, the morning of July 4th. Back home in the U.S., fireworks, picnics, and BBQs mark the national holiday. We were taken aback when the orchestra that was playing in the cemetery starting playing the U.S. national anthem, and everyone, regardless of country of origin, stopped. Some took off their hats, hung their heads and put their hands together in prayer or over their hearts. Many wept.

Hudson and I put our hands over our hearts and looked at the American flag flapping overhead. We both felt emotional — for the day, for the events of this place and for the emotions of our fellow travelers.

Before the song was completed, the applause started and continued to the end. Aside from the U.S. national anthem, I think I can only recognize two, maybe three, other countries' anthems. This makes me feel proud to be an American, and slightly ignorant of the rest of the world.

As Hudson becomes a citizen of the world, so shall I.

We signed up for the free guided tour of the cemetery. The tour guide, a witty British man, introduced himself to the crowd and asked people where they were from. To the Americans, he joked that he didn't understand what all the July 4th fuss was about. As he walked through the cemetery with us, he shared stories of the war and the big picture. Occasionally he would pause at a grave and talk about that specific soldier.

Marked with crosses or Stars of David, the graves showed the name and rank of each soldier and their dates of life. Some of the graves said, "Here rests in honored glory a comrade in arms known but to God." The guide pointed out three Medals of Honor, one of which had been given to Theodore Roosevelt, Jr.

"The five beach invasion included the Americans taking Utah and Omaha. The Canadians took Juno, and the British captured Gold and Sword. Everything that could go wrong that day, did," he said.

He pointed to a bluff that dropped down from the cemetery to the beach.

"You and I can walk down that bluff in under 10 minutes," he said. "On June 6, 1944, it took the Allies two hours to get that far."

A quiet moment passed, allowing us to absorb his words. Waving his arm over the gravesites, he said, "Almost 10,000 soldiers are buried here. All facing west."

He paused, then finished, "Facing home."

From the tour, we walked to and through the museum. Five hours later, we left. We were full of knowledge, pride and emotion. However, something was missing.

There was nothing to buy, nothing for sale. No distractions or merchandised nostalgia. This place was unfiltered. It was the first time I heard myself say, "It was a place with a feeling." Even now, years later when I recall that day, I get goosebumps.

Accounts of that day have been well-written and portrayed in countless books. However, seeing and feeling it live has so much more power and impact. It is a pilgrimage I would recommend for all Americans to experience at least once in their lifetime.

We ate dinner in the casually elegant hotel restaurant that night. Hudson successfully hung a dessert spoon off his nose for an extended period of time. It was the levity we needed after a powerful day.

After an emotional stay visiting the beaches of Normandy, our next adventure took us south, to the border of Brittany. I was thankful finding the D572 to St. Lô was easy as we set out on our own pilgrimage to Mont St. Michel.

We had done some reading about "Le Mont," as Hudson called it. Le Mont had more than 1,000 years of history to share. It was fascinating to learn how this chunk of granite was developed, as well as the effect of Christianity on the area. Named for Archangel Michael, it was the site of Christian pilgrimages for years. There were countless accounts of miracles. But what we were most excited to witness and experience were the tides.

Le Mont, the monastery, built into the granite slab, sits like a Hershey kiss in the middle of mud. We read that the tides surrounding the area are among the fastest in the world.

When we first saw Le Mont off in the distance, it was like a mirage, ethereal and surprising. I pulled the car off the road the first chance I could, to get out and just look at it.

Hudson snapped a few pictures and we drove a little further and repeated the same movements. It was unbelievable to see in the distance — Oz-like and dreamy.

"The first thing I want to do when we get there," Hudson said, "is go walking in the mud flats."

No cars are allowed on Le Mont, so we parked on the causeway. Wheeling our suitcases up the stony walkway, we checked into the Terrasses Poulard, our hotel for two nights. Our room was up a few stone steps. It was a sweet suite with shuttered windows.

Staircases and feathers were everywhere. We left our unopened bags in the room and headed for the flats. Seagulls flew overhead. The tide was rolling in, and it was fast. Hudson and I climbed the rocks and soon our feet and hands were muddy. Many people were taking advantage of the focal point, marveling at the speed of the water, pouring in from three rivers coming together.

Seagulls and little beach birds that reminded me of wrens outnumbered the people. Soon the water pushed us back to the rocks and onto the stone walkway.

At the highest point, Archangel Michael stands on a peak, watching over Le Mont. We photographed him at all angles. His gold wings shimmered in the sun until it finally set at 10:30 p.m.

It was an island made completely of stone, with tiny steps everywhere. Some led to windowed lookouts, while others led to narrow alleyways. We walked the island easily, pointing out all the dogs.

It seemed the people traveling with dogs outnumbered the people without. We were missing our dog Chase, a schipperke, who was staying with friends.

On a rock balcony, we walked into a couple with their pregnant bulldog.

We nodded and said, "Hi."

They seemed friendly, and we asked about their dog.

"She is pregnant," they told us, and asked where we were from.

"America," Hudson answered, petting the dog.

"Where are you from?" I asked them.

"Belgium. This is our first time to Mont St. Michel," they said.

"Ours, too. We were just talking about how many people travel with their dogs here," I said.

"She goes everywhere with us," they said, smiling. "And will after she has the puppies."

"We have a schipperke, named Chase, at home," Hudson said. "Schipperkes are Belgian, too."

We made small talk for a while, and they told us they thought we were Dutch when we first approached them. It was the second time while in France that we were told we looked Dutch.

From Mont St. Michel, we drove to Rouen and back to Paris to the airport. On the flight home we recapped our trip and how much we learned about France and loved the French culture. We both said the highlight was July 4th in Normandy.

Success — my first solo trans-Atlantic flight with Hudson! I felt excited, confident, reflective and very lucky to be able to do this with him at this age. All the reading could not match the real-life experience.

"Mom, where are we going next year?" Hudson asked as the plane left Charles de Gaulle airport.

Chapter 5

Morocco

When the driver picked us up at the Casablanca airport, his eyes and smile were very warm, welcoming and professional. He gave us his card. "Abdellatif Chakir" it read.

I read the card and looked up at him. Just as I was about to ask how to pronounce his name, he said, "Call me Chakir. Like your Shaquille O'Neal in America."

We talked about hotel details and driving specifics, and then we were silent.

"What do you want from your trip?" Chakir asked.

"I want to feel it," I answered.

He looked at me, studying my face.

"Really feel it?" he countered. I felt there was a buffet offering here in Morocco. There were multi-level selections from light and lively, surface glazing, to something deeper and more significant.

"Yes. Really feel it," I said. "I am a tourist and want to see the touristy areas. But I also want to see and feel the real Morocco."

He listened intently, looking at me seriously measuring the weight of my words.

"Okay. I will take you to the Berber Village," he answered, and smiled.

"Bring candy," he said and winked at Hudson.

Chakir was soft and solid at the same time. Everything physical about him was light brown — skin, eyes and hair. He walked slowly. He was intensely aware and very calm. As he guided us through questions, he shared that his father was a tour driver as well. He used to accompany him on some of his outings. Chakir obviously knew and loved his native country.

If intuition could be personified, it would be Chakir. There was a knowingness about him. He said, "Inshallah" a lot. He taught us the meaning — God willing. When we asked questions or made comments, his answers and comments were often punctuated with "Inshallah."

Arriving in Marrakech, Chakir walked with us for a while. We ate juicy prickly pears while walking through the souks or marketplaces of Marrakech. Hudson and I marveled at the perfection of the conical mountains of earth-toned spices. Then we found a candy store.

Hudson picked up a large, colorful bag of Jolly Ranchers and said, "We can bring these to the Berber Village, mom."

Jolly Ranchers. We smiled for the familiarity of the hard, brightly colored red, orange, green, and blue candy. In elementary school, Hudson was awarded many Jolly Ranchers for assignments, projects, and extra credit.

"Great idea," I said.

The decision to hire someone else to drive us through two weeks in Morocco was based on a few factors. First, it was inexpensive. The dollar-to-dirham exchange worked in our favor, $1:8 dirham. Having someone else drive meant I could read, look out the window, relax and talk with Hudson, or just shut my eyes and not worry about getting us from place to place. Additionally, I don't speak Arabic, so reading road signs would have presented another challenge, and frustration.

Also, I am a woman. I didn't want to be so naïve to assume a single woman traveling with her son would be accepted. So we made arrangements to hire Chakir, and he picked us up in the hotel lobby in Marrakech. Hudson and I jumped into the backseats of the van and showed him the bag of Jolly Ranchers.

"Is this okay?" Hudson asked.

"That is perfect," Chakir smiled.

As we drove past dusty tan camels sitting on the sidewalks, Chakir told us Marrakech is called the red city, as all the buildings are a terracotta color.

There was a heaviness in the air from heat and dust, and it seemed to subtly suggest that we slow down.

We asked about the camels.

"Actually, camels have two humps and dromedaries have just one. Those are dromedaries over there," he finished, pointing to the kneeling animals on the sidewalk, tied to a nearby tree with a rope.

"Are they for decoration?" I asked.

"They are there for the tourists to ride," he answered. "Hudson, do you want to ride a dromedary while you are in Morocco?"

Hudson looked at me for approval. I nodded. And Hudson said excitedly, "Okay."

"Okay. Tomorrow you will take a ride," Chakir said.

The city of Marrakech, once the capital of Morocco, sits at the base of the southern Atlas Mountains. The Atlas Mountains cover more than 1,600 miles and continue west into Algeria and Tunisia.

We gazed at the Atlas Mountains through the front windshield. They looked like a brown crumbled paper bag. During the hour-long ride to the Berber Village, we gradually climbed. We passed occasional roadside stands selling tagines.

Tagines were everywhere in Morocco. The heavy clay pottery was often painted and glazed. The flat base was covered with a cone or dome, and served as a slow-cooker for lambs and other meats. Often used for cooking stews, smaller tagines were used to hold oils and spices.

"Most Moroccans can claim Berber heritage," Chakir said. "And most of the population of the Atlas Mountains is Berber. They are the original people here. They are like your Native Americans."

The van drove up the mountainside. We looked out and saw a narrow, rocky river. There were several young boys swimming and splashing.

"Get your candy ready," Chakir said as he parked the van in front of an earthen adobe house.

We stepped out onto the hardened dirt street. There were pale, rough-textured adobe two-story buildings on either side. Chakir walked a few steps ahead, leading the way. As we turned a corner, we narrowly avoided bumping into a short woman in her 70s wearing a dress. She was walking while two goats followed directly behind her.

She smiled as she walked past. Chakir said, "That's barley on her back." Now we knew why the goats were following so closely. They were eating and walking with her!

"The crops that the Berber people grow, like the barley you just saw, are ones that can grow in high altitudes — corn and maize and turnips and potatoes."

He stopped speaking as a young boy of six or seven ran up. He stood close, as though he was joining us. Dark brown hair and darker eyes with thick black eyelashes looked up at us hopefully.

"Hudson, where are those candies?" Chakir asked.

Hudson took the candies out of the bag.

"Why don't you offer him one?" Chakir suggested.

Hudson reached in the bag and took out a red Jolly Rancher and handed it to the boy, who took it and ran away as quickly as he had appeared.

Within moments, three more young boys under the age of ten appeared and stood close to Hudson.

No words were spoken. Hudson reached in and pulled out three candies, handing one to each boy. They ran away, spread the word, and soon a pack appeared.

I looked at Chakir, searching his face for a clue to what was going on.

Chakir was gentle and strong with the kids. He smiled warmly and had a comfortable, yet authoritarian way about him.

Ten boys stood with their hands extended, including a tiny three or four-year old. Once they each had a Jolly Rancher they ran away.

Hudson and I looked at each other and smiled.

"Mom, it's the Fibonacci sequence," he said as more boys approached, hands extended. The Fibonacci sequence is a series of numbers that create a pattern by adding the previous number to the current one; so 0,1,1,2,3,5,8,13,21,34.

After every child in the village had a Jolly Rancher, they all hung around and followed us.

One boy, about nine or ten years old walked up and stood close to me.

"Money," he said looking at me extending his hand.

"Chakir," I said, "I have a pocket full of coins. Is it okay to give out money?"

Chakir turned around and gave a hard look at the boy, which sent him walking away.

"Think about what you teach them if you do that, Laura," he said and walked ahead of us.

Chakir was right. To give them money was to enable them and teach them to beg. So I did not give them money, just smiles.

We walked on. I asked Chakir to take our picture with the boys, all of us squeezed together. As Chakir took the shot, I felt someone touching my rear end. I looked at the boy next to me and he said something in Berber to his friend on my other side.

Chakir approached and spoke harshly to the boy who had touched me. I don't know what he said, but the boy, about twelve or thirteen, shrunk back and put his hands together under his chin and looked ashamed. He looked at the ground.

"Would you like to go inside a Berber home and have some Moroccan whiskey?" Chakir offered, smiling.

The reference to whiskey brought a smile to my face and Hudson's. At an earlier stop, we drank Moroccan whiskey at an outdoor café. Chakir told us Moroccan whiskey is mint tea. Served hot, the amber-colored tea resembles swamp water or whiskey, and is packed with mint leaves.

"Yes, that sounds great," we answered. We said goodbye to the boys and followed Chakir.

The street was hard-packed with light tan dirt and bowed in the middle. On either side was a natural gutter that transported water, sewage and organic material.

We heard bleating and mooing and smelled animals.

"Here we are," Chakir said.

We stood before a home that looked like it was from the Bible. Open-air windows exposed humble rooms with nothing synthetic or non-essential. The home was organic inside and out, authentic with rooms and furniture that had purpose. No distractions of frivolity or show.

"The animals live downstairs and the people live upstairs," Chakir explained.

Inside a small arched opening were a group of chickens. A goat was tied to a wooden post nearby. Rabbits were in another contained area. We walked up exterior steps into the home.

Waiting for us in the living room was the hosting Berber family. The husband and wife and their son and daughter smiled warmly when we entered.

The son stepped forward.

"Hi, I am Mohammed. Welcome to our home. Would you like some Moroccan whiskey?" he asked.

His smile was kind and inviting and I felt at ease with his manner. I also felt he was the family ambassador and the most confident in dealing with new people. Muslim culture places a high value on hospitality, and their friendly open manner made us feel right at home.

"Please," I said, and sat on the three-seat sofa with Hudson by my side.

"With sugar or without?" he asked.

Before I could answer, Chakir advised ordering it without sugar.

"Otherwise you will have teeth like a Moroccan," he laughed.

A few days earlier, Chakir had pointed out a smiling man who was missing a few teeth, the remaining ones were brownish in color.

"See his teeth?" he had said. "That's why you drink Moroccan whiskey without sugar."

I smiled at Chakir and said to Mohammed, "Without, thanks."

As Mohammed prepared the tea, the rest of his family left the room. We waited quietly. I studied the sofa upholstery. It was ornate with a white ground and embroidered green vines with red flowers and seemed to be the only decoration in the home. Two side chairs sat to the right and left of the sofa, creating a vignette. Centered between the furniture was a wooden coffee table, and that was where our Moroccan whiskey was placed.

"My family only speaks Berber," Mohammed said, placing the tea on the table.

"Please tell them thank you for welcoming us into their home," I replied.

"Many of the people that live here have never left this village," Chakir explained. "They live here and go to school here. Mohammed speaks seven languages."

"Seven languages?" I repeated. "How did you learn seven languages?" I stopped myself from saying *here*.

"I learn from the tourists that visit us here. I can speak Berber, English, French, German, Spanish, Arabic and a little Hebrew," he offered.

He smiled as he pulled an iPhone out of his back pocket.

"I even speak American," he said, dropping his head down, pretending to use the iPhone.

He laughed when he looked up at us.

The air was warm. Occasionally the smell of the farm animals below wafted through the living room. There was a stillness and calmness in Morocco, a quietness that was not awkward. A quiet so palpable, that I could actually hear, smell, taste, see and feel with heightened intensity. We sipped on Moroccan whiskey in this comfortable quiet, humble place.

"Would you like to see the kitchen?" Mohammed asked.

"Sure," I answered, nodding.

Hudson and I walked six feet to the opening of the kitchen. Mohammed's mother and sister smiled and nodded and took a step back. It was obvious they did not want to speak, but even without words it was still a comfortable setting.

The monastic, dirt-floored kitchen was utilitarian. It reminded me of the Tenement Museum in New York City's lower east side. There was a stove and a sink and a small table with four chairs.

"My sister does henna, Laura," Mohammed said. "Would you like to have her paint henna on your hand?"

"Sure," I replied, and smiled at Hudson.

"She can paint henna on Hudson's arm, too," he offered.

Hudson nodded and sat next to Mohammed's sister. We both watched as she took out a white sack that was used for decorating cakes.

She quietly and calmly decorated Hudson's upper arm, then moved next to me.

I have never had a henna tattoo. When she took my left arm and laid it on one of the pillows from the sofa, I looked up at her face and shrugged. She smiled and patted my arm. "Relax," she seemed to say.

Gently and deliberately she squeezed the thick, green pesto-like organic material onto my hand.

Chakir, Hudson, and Mohammed left the room.

"Let me show you how we take a shower here," I heard Mohammed saying to Hudson, and then they were gone.

Later, Hudson told me the shower was a homemade enclosure that looked like a space ship. It had a silver tent with a bucket of water nearby.

Seated close, the smell of the henna mix was inescapable. Mohammed's sister was deft and precisely squeezed the mixture out of a tiny syringe needle onto my hand and arm. Both our eyes fixed on the pattern and occasionally we looked up and gave each other a Mona Lisa smile. She spoke only Berber and I only spoke English, and yet I felt so much communication between us.

As I watched her craft the ornate organic pattern on my hand, my hand started to blend with the upholstery of the sofa. The same vine-like floral pattern that was on the sofa was on my hand.

I lifted my eyes to re-adjust. Then something happened to me that had never happened before. I looked off in the distance and became aware of my breathing. As I did this I had a deep knowing. I knew two things.

One, I would be here, in this village and in this house again, sometime in the future. This came as a surprise to me. I prefer to see and experience new places, not revisit places.

The second premonition was an image. It was a future scene of this Berber living room. I was looking into the living room and not invited to sit down. The home was now a museum. I felt a wave of emotion and my eyes watered. This clear image was in the near future. It meant the Berber people were being pushed out.

I turned to face Mohammed's sister. Could she see or feel the change in me? She didn't look up as she continued to drag the henna mixture over my hand. I looked down at my hand to see if it had changed. My hand had become an extension of the textile.

She completed the artwork with a smile face on my pointer finger. She looked up at me and we both smiled and nodded.

Rabat

Aaaaarrrroooooooohhhhh

"Mom, what is that sound?" Hudson asked.

"I don't know, it sounds like an air siren," I said.

We walked toward the window. Opening the shutters we stuck our heads out in the night, toward the direction of the sound.

Aaaaarrrroooooooohhhhh

It was 10 pm. We had checked into the Dar Mayssane riad in the capital city of Rabat earlier that afternoon. A riad is a traditional

Moroccan house or palace. An open-air interior garden or courtyard is the defining feature.

When we arrived earlier that afternoon, Chakir parked the van at the end of the street. We wheeled our suitcases past a "No Cars Past This Point" sign. The narrow street was unadorned. On either side of us were plain sand-colored exterior walls with very few windows.

"Here we are," Chakir stopped in front of a large, dark wooden door. He reached for the doorknocker in its center and slowly and deliberately knocked. Just above the knocker was a hand.

"Why is there a hand on the door?" Hudson asked, looking at Chakir.

"That is the hand of Fatima, Hudson. Many Moroccans put it on a door to keep away evil. It's there for protection," Chakir explained.

The door opened and we were transformed.

We stepped over a raised threshold into a jewelry box.

We had read about riads and how they were inward focused, both physically and metaphorically. The center courtyard and garden create a common focal point, while the virtually windowless exterior provides the family privacy and protection.

Once inside, I stopped. I was stunned.

"Wow! Wow. It's beautiful in here," I said with unbridled enthusiasm. "What a surprise!"

The transition from the plain, modest exterior to the colorful, dynamic interior was powerful. Although our suitcases were being brought in and we were to check-in, I just stood there.

I looked up and discovered a cedar ceiling engraved and painted with a highly flourished pattern of vines and flowers. The wood planks were mounted in a high/low pattern, giving the vines a three-dimensional depth. My eyes moved to the corner and down the wall. A band of wooden fretwork mounted at the top of the wall transitioned into a warm white Venetian plaster, glazed and mottled. I'd learned that Venetian plaster provides a dehumidifying effect.

Halfway down the wall, the Venetian plaster met cobalt blue, sunflower yellow, and white 3x3 mosaic tiles. The tiles cascaded and continued onto the floor, where my eye finally stopped scanning to see my suitcase being wheeled ahead of me.

"This way, please."

As we turned the corner, the courtyard appeared in front of us. Small potted trees and floppy leafed plants sat next to pots and vases of bright pink and red flowers. The transition from hallway to courtyard was framed with a floor-to-ceiling drape cinched with a sash. The scent of fresh flowers mingled with the aroma of our future dinner.

We were directed to sit in a small seating vignette.

"Wait until you see your room," Chakir said, smiling.

We were told to follow the rose petals. Hudson and I exchanged looks.

The host extended his hand, directing us through the courtyard. At the base of the tiled steps, a puddle of red rose petals was strewn. The subtle rose scent wafted through the air as we walked upstairs to our room.

Red rose petals were scattered all over the top of the white matelassé bed cover. The bed was so high Hudson had to throw his body onto it. Cobalt blue, yellow and white mosaics adorned the walls here as well. The cedar ceiling was ornately engraved.

Just outside the bathroom there was another spiral staircase. At the top of the stairs was a claw-foot tub. A large open window revealed the city of Rabat.

The bathrooms are different and interesting when we travel. There was no vertical shower so we sat in the tub and used the extendable hose to wash and shower, leaving the whole room wet.

The next morning, we ate breakfast in the open-air courtyard. Occasionally two birds swooped past, looking for crumbs. Our plans for the day included visiting the Chellah ruins and the Mohammed V mausoleum. We were reading our travel guide when the riad host walked over.

"How did you sleep last night?" he looked first at me and then Hudson.

"The room is beautiful and we slept so well," I started. "But we do have a question. We heard a siren last night and weren't sure what it was."

"That was the fifth and final call to prayer," he answered. "The mosque is not far from here. The call is broadcasted through loudspeakers."

The call to prayer is one of the five pillars of Islam, the religion of Muslims. Five times a day, believers are called, in this case by siren, to pray. Prayers are said facing Mecca in Saudi Arabia. It is the holiest city of Islam and the birthplace of the prophet, Muhammad. Muslims believe Allah spoke to him and those words became the Qur'an.

A pilgrimage to Mecca, at least once in a lifetime, is another pillar of Islam. The pillars are basic acts and considered mandatory. They include believing in one God, Allah; offering alms; and fasting, from dawn to dusk, during Ramadan.

Regardless where they are located in the world, they face Mecca and the Masjid al-Haram, the largest mosque in the world, to pray.

Essaouira

The best conversation I had while in Morocco happened in Essaouira. It was after the long, dusty drive on the desert road heading west into the Atlantic breeze.

With Marrakech and the Atlas Mountains behind us, the landscape ahead was a flat tan line with only an occasional break. Road signs and groves of argan trees were the only vertical break during the two-hour ride to the seaside town of Essaouira. Studying the tree line, we knew which way the Atlantic Ocean was by the angle of the trees. Slanting from the wind, their gnarled bases held strong in the dry desert dirt. The green treetops featured a messy array of leaves, nuts, and goats.

The day, like all the days in Morocco, was sunny, very hot, and dry. We sat in the back seat of Chakir's van, anticipating our next adventure.

Looking in the rearview mirror at Hudson, Chakir asked, "Do you want to see monkeys in trees?"

We had seen a monkey in the Jemaa el-Fna square back in Marrakech. The tiled, open-aired marketplace was full of music, with vendors selling tagines and artisans displaying hand-crafted jewelry. Seated on a red and gold Persian rug was a man with a tailless monkey. He waved Hudson and me over. He placed the monkey, who was wearing a red velvet vest, on Hudson's head.

"Monkeys in trees?" Hudson repeated. We exchanged surprised looks in the back seat.

Pointing out the passenger window, Chakir said, "Look over there."

We both looked out at the grove of argan trees.

Then we saw them.

Goats!

Chakir pulled the van over to the side of the road. We sprung out of the back seat and ran toward the tree. There were goats in it.

"What is this?" I said, not recognizing my own voice.

Overhead, full-grown goats were perched on branches, munching the leaves of the large tree. The dozen or so goats stood confidently on branches ten or twelve feet above my head. As captivated as we were by them, they ignored our presence.

"Goats are good climbers," Chakir started. "They climb onto the argan tree and eat the leaves, as you can see."

Three men with skin the color of iodine suddenly appeared from the grove. I hesitated, looking at Chakir for assurance that this was normal and it was okay for us to be there. Chakir picked up on my alarm. He nodded and smiled, letting me know we were safe.

"They are the farmers," he said. "They have something for you to hold, Laura."

In their rough, outstretched hands was a docile. black and white baby goat. They handed it to me.

To my surprise, I accepted it without question.

They smiled, revealing those Moroccan teeth Chakir had warned us about. I silently thanked Chakir for advising us to always select the sugarless version of Moroccan whiskey.

As I stood holding the baby goat, the adult goats overhead continued to eat. One of the smiling farmers hoisted Hudson onto a low branch.

They all stepped back and Chakir took our picture.

That picture was our 2011 Christmas card. "Location is Decoration" was the message.

Waving and smiling at the three farmers, we walked back to the van. As we drove away, one man with an especially toothy grin gave Hudson thumbs up. Hudson smiled back and gave thumbs up in return.

"What did you think, Hudson?" Chakir asked.

"That was great!" Hudson answered enthusiastically.

We drove for a short while talking animatedly about the goats in trees. How did they stay perched on small branches? How did they climb the tree? How did they get down?

Overhearing our questions, Chakir asked if we wanted to learn more about the argan tree and nuts. We told him we did, and he suggested a second stop on the way to Essaouira.

Chakir slowed down and pulled into a dirt parking lot, stirring up dust. Once the air cleared, we saw a black dog sleeping under an argan tree.

Opening the van door, we stepped out and saw a plain single-story building with a sign: "Women's Cooperative."

"You will learn more about the argan tree and nut, here," Chakir said. "Let's go inside and I will introduce you to a woman who can take you on a tour."

We followed Chakir into the clean, quiet building. A middle-aged woman walked into the entryway from another room and smiled when she saw Chakir. They spoke a few words in Arabic.

Chakir said, "I will meet you outside at the picnic table, after the tour."

We followed the tour guide into a room. Women were seated on the floor in an assembly line of activity.

"The co-op is for women who are having or who have had some hardships in life. They are paid for their time and efforts," the young tour guide said.

She didn't offer any examples, and I examined the women seated on the floor, trying to discern what their individual hardships were.

Seated cross-legged on the floor, their long skirts stretched taut across their thighs, the women worked from their created work surface. We stood and watched them. The first woman broke the argan nut between two stones and placed it into a brown wooden bowl.

The argan nut is orange-brown in color and oval or conical in shape, the size of an America quarter. The hard shell cracks to reveal a white, fleshy interior and oil.

The woman seated to our guide's left took the bowl of broken shells and removed the nut within. She placed her nuts into a brown bowl, which was passed to the left. The next woman took the nuts and ground them creating a thick, goopy, molasses-looking liquid.

There were no men in the co-op. After we observed the women working, we were led to a showroom. In the showroom we were urged to try the oils. A plate of cut pita bread sat next to the bowls of oils.

We tried them all. The cooking and peanut oils were our favorites. Both bottles were 750ml and cost a total of 440 dirham (about $55). Heavy in texture, nutty and distinct in taste, the argan nut products are high in vitamin E and antioxidants. Argan oil can be used in skin, hair and nail products.

Though the price was a little high, we were buying an authentic and healthy product. Plus we were keeping the women inside working.

The tour guide asked me to extend my hand. When I did, she

squeezed a white blop of argan lotion into my palm. It had a strong organic smell, not perfumey. My hands felt smooth and not oily. I bought a bottle of that, too.

After paying for the oils and lotion, we rejoined Chakir. Seated at the picnic table outside, he was drinking Moroccan whiskey. A bowl of pita bread and dipping argan oil were in the middle of the table.

We joined him and shared the bread and oil.

Morocco was slow, warm, sensual and kind, and so much of our enjoyment of the country was because of Chakir. His down-to-earth manner and calm directives made me feel, as a single mother, calm, safe and in excellent hands. He was the best ambassador to his country. He shared a few stories about his two children, and his wife who was pregnant with their third child. At one point during our trip, he said he had spoken to his wife and she told him their third baby would be a girl.

With each city we toured, he made the transition smooth, seemingly effortless and friendly. Essaouira (pron: Swearrra, roll the r) was no different. He parked the van in a municipal lot and guided us to the harbor area.

Essaouira juts out into the Atlantic Ocean. It is a Kasbah, or fortress. A fortified city. There was a steady warm breeze. From where we stood with Chakir we could see ramparts, or defending walls, decorated with parapets. In front of us, cobalt blue fishing boats jammed the harbor. The fore, or front, of the boats were designed and built higher than the aft, to push through ocean waves.

In every city we visited, Chakir asked if we wanted to walk with a hired tour guide. We said yes in every city. As we waited to meet our Essaouira tour guide, Chakir told us about the fishing off the coastline.

"A lot of Spanish fishermen come down here to fish for sardines," as he spoke, a woman in a white floppy hat approached.

"Rasheeda, this is Laura and her son, Hudson," Chakir made the introduction.

"Hi Rasheeda, nice to meet you," Hudson and I spoke in unison.

Rasheeda was about my height (5'7"). She had one hand on top of her floppy white hat, to keep it on her head in the persistent breeze. She was dressed in a traditional Moroccan loose-fitting, white, flowing dress over pants, and her tan face and smile were warm and intelligent. Her brown eyes were heavily lidded.

With every introduction to the city tour guide, Chakir removed himself and told us he would connect with us at the end of the walk.

Making easy conversation, Rasheeda asked us about our trip. We walked toward the historical center, the medina. She stopped at an arched entryway and pointed up.

"This is the entry to the medina of Essaouira," she said. "This is the Gate of Tolerance. At the top of the arch are the symbols of the three great religions."

Looking up, we saw the Star of David, the Islamic moon and star and the Christian cross.

"Essaouira has a long history of diversity and peaceful coexistence between different ethnic groups. The city is well designed, as it was planned before it was developed. It is set up in a grid, like New York City," she explained as we slowly walked along the cobbled streets.

Rasheeda slowly walked the narrow streets with Hudson and me next to her or slightly behind her. In all the medinas of Morocco there were no cars, no vehicles at all, only pedestrians. The medinas were maze-like, and the winding narrow alley ways often brought us to a souk or market.

"First, we will go to the fish market and then we will go to the ramparts through the Jewish Quarter. One request," she said, and we looked over at her. "Please feel free to take pictures of any of the scenery, but not the people. They feel they are on display when they are simply doing what their lives require them to do. If you were home doing what you do on a normal day you would not want to feel like you are so strange that someone would take a picture of you. Right?"

We nodded, and agreed. We took a lot of pictures of a lot of cats.

Cats were everywhere. They were friendly and, judging by their plump bodies, well fed. Throughout our time in Morocco, we saw more cats than people. They are beloved. Serving a higher purpose, they kept rodents at bay. Bowls of water and food were out, everywhere. We stopped to pet a few of the cats. Rasheeda told us they were taken care of by the government of Morocco, and were spayed and neutered.

We stopped and stooped down to pet a kitten. Rasheeda said, "We take care of our animals. However, dogs are not allowed in our homes. They are considered unsanitary."

Rasheeda walked us through the fish market, which was sloshy and wet. We were thankful for the unrelenting breeze, as it lifted the smell of fish in 100+ degree heat. Hoses, ice and buckets of water were everywhere. I walked looking down so as not to trip over anything. The only thing more abundant than the fish on display were the cats.

Fish, spices, grains and cats. We walked past a slanted table covered in chipped ice, partially exposing enormous eels. A steady stream of water drained off the table onto the cobblestones. When we stopped to look, Rasheeda told us they were baby eels.

We strolled winding, tight streets, past bright white walls with chalky cerulean blue doors and window frames. The contrast from the fish market was fresh and startling and felt so right for an ocean city. The air was salty and misty, and I could smell the sea.

"At one time, forty percent of the population of Essaouira was Jewish," Rasheeda said as we walked towards the mellah, or Jewish quarter. "There are very few Jews still living in Essaouira and even fewer reminders of their presence here at one time."

Essaouira had been a thriving port city with connections to Europe. Many Jews began emigrating after the formation of Israel in 1948 and after the Six Day War in 1967.

Walking and talking with Rasheeda was slow and easy, she shared her insights and wisdom on Morocco life, people and time. Essaouira was enchanting. We talked about what it would be like for non-Moroccans to live there.

"You can buy a home here if you are not Moroccan, and not pay taxes for 10 years," she explained.

I started to interrupt, incredulous at the idea. She held up her hand and continued. "However," she said emphatically, pausing for effect, "you must help five Moroccans with work."

She told us many people buy real estate there. It was relatively inexpensive, she said.

"We can build it," she said pointing to a dilapidated crumbled former home, "but we don't maintain it."

Walking through the mellah, she occasionally paused so we could take pictures of the architecture and the views of the Atlantic Ocean. We walked into the breeze towards the ramparts overlooking the Atlantic.

On the ramparts looking at the sea, Rasheeda stopped walking. She allowed us to take in the view of the sea and city.

It was a quiet, reflective moment and I said, "I love your country, it is beautiful, serene and the people are so kind. This has been a great experience for Hudson, and me. It is important for him to see other parts of the world and for me, it has been transformative."

She nodded slowly and said, "Yes, as a white American boy it is important for your son to see other ways of life."

When she said "white American boy" Hudson looked at me in shock.

"Mom, did you tell her?" Hudson said to me.

"Everything I have said to Rasheeda, you have heard," I answered.

Looking at Rasheeda, I explained, "I often refer to Hudson as my white American boy, top of the heap. What do you do when your child has been born with so many advantages? What do they strive for?"

"It is important for him to see the world, not just the American perspective," she offered.

I nodded.

"Yes, we can be 'American-centric.' Hudson will benefit as a boy, and as an American, to see how much we have there, and how much there is out here. He will appreciate the abundance he has been born into. I think when you are at the top of the heap, you need to give back. Do service. Just not in the military."

We stood quietly for a moment.

Camera in hand, Hudson wandered over to the cannons and parapets and took pictures.

Rasheeda looked at me.

"Laura, what have you learned in Morocco?" she asked.

I looked at Rasheeda and said, "Ahmed, the city tour guide in Marrakech, said something that was interesting and thought-provoking. Something I want to believe."

Listening, she asked, "What did he say?"

"Like you, he asked what had we learned and enjoyed so far in Morocco," I started. "I told him one of the surprises in Morocco was the architecture and interiors."

Briefly, I explained that selling to architects and interior designers had been my career for more than two decades.

"I told Ahmed how I loved that the outside, the exterior of the buildings were modest and unassuming and very plain. They completely hid the beauty, color, and nuanced subtleties of the interiors. I admired that all the materials on the inside were real. The interiors were authentic, not just decorative."

Rasheeda patiently listened as I continued.

"I told him I was especially impressed by the Rabat riad. I thought it was one of the most transformative physical transitions, from outside to inside."

We both glanced over at Hudson taking pictures of the ocean waves.

"Rasheeda, when I told Ahmed how moved I was, he scared me," I offered.

"Scared you?" she seemed surprised.

We both stood facing Hudson in the distance, with the warm ocean breeze caressing our faces.

"When I told him about how much I loved the surprise of the beauty of the interior, he squared off on me and stepped closer," I said, and showed her what I meant. I stepped into our invisible space and stood directly and firmly in front of her.

She nodded and listened.

I continued, "He said, 'what you have just described, the modest outside and the beautiful inside; that is how we view our women. They do not flash their beauty to the world; they show it only to their husbands and family.'"

Examining her face for a reaction, I said, "Rasheeda, when he told me that I scoffed and gave him this look," I stepped back, tilted my head, raised my eyebrows and gave a look of disdain.

"I told him, 'really, that's how you look at your women? Because it seems oppressive, coming from where I live. I would like to believe what you said, because it is quite poetic, but my impression of your culture makes me think otherwise,'" I told Rasheeda.

Rasheeda studied me. I was sure, woman to woman, she would agree. She surprised me with her response.

"Laura," she started, "That was the most significant thing you learned in Morocco so far?"

I felt immediately embarrassed and self-conscious. I wished I had said something loftier, something about the Atlas Mountains or souks or Islam.

Looking at Rasheeda, I said, in a quieter confessional tone, "It is."

I did not feel judgment from her, just that quiet patience.

Then she said, "Your culture is the opposite. You are looked at from the outside in."

Nodding slowly, I agreed.

I thought about the culture I grew up and live in and felt the truth of what she said. Big cars, big houses, a lot of show. But what I thought about most was women. In the United States, women were decorated and valued for their outer look, rather than their inner essence.

The conversations with Ahmed and later with Rasheeda stayed with me. I found myself contemplating how girls and women are raised and treated.

When I was young, elementary school-aged, I was my father's daughter. I just wanted to please him and make him happy. When he was angry it scared me, so I would do anything to avoid making him mad. My self-image was centered in what he saw in me. I acted the way he wanted me to. I played sports, was a tomboy, talked about things that interested him. It wasn't until college that my mother's influence grabbed hold of me.

Rasheeda's words hit me hard as I saw not only my culture through her eyes, but I saw myself. And I felt like a phony.

Hammam

The warmth of Morocco was epitomized in the hammam. From Arabic, the word means to heat or spread warmth. A weekly cleansing ritual, hammam is a communal public bath. Moroccans go to the hammam to refresh, rejuvenate and socialize. They stay for two to three hours per visit. There are separate entrances for men and women, and the cost is minimal.

When we returned from Essaouira, Chakir brought us to the Riad Kniza, a hammam in the Derb El Guernaoui Hotel in Marrakech. Parking near a souk, we made our way past fruit and spice vendors. We followed Chakir down an alley where a young Moroccan boy was playing with a soccer ball. He kicked the black and white ball to Chakir who kicked it to Hudson.

A few steps later, Chakir opened a door. We were transformed yet again.

The first thing that struck me was the smell of the hammam, the scent of oils heavy in the dimly lit calm space. Peaceful and serene, the interior was unadorned and immaculate. I heard trickling water in the humid waiting room as I took in the simple and exotic interior. It was quiet except for the sound of the water and an occasional slippered woman shuffling by.

Chakir left us. Hudson and I were led to a locker room and told to undress. Two white cotton bath robes hung on a nearby peg. On the floor, under the robes, were two pairs of colorful leather sandals known as babouches.

Hudson, ten at the time, was with me in the locker room. We were the only ones there.

When we walked out of the locker room, Saida, the hammam hostess, met us in the dimly lit hallway. Down the corridor, an arched opening revealed a shallow pool. We were enveloped by lit candles, low lighting and complete silence. The hammam felt peaceful.

Saida, dressed in a thin cotton sarong, her skin shiny and wet, led us into a steam room.

Typically, the men and women take hammam separately, but Hudson was considered a child at the time and so we took hammam together.

The steam room was one material, white marble. Two marble slabs were positioned against the wall. A lone shower head was in the center back wall, the floor was wet and the lighting was soft. We stood waiting for direction.

Saida took our robes and instructed us to kick off the babouches.

We did and stood naked in the middle of the room. She turned up the steam and the room filled instantly with warm moist air. With little visibility, we shuffled to the white marble slabs. Hudson was sent to the right and I was sent to the left. Saida laid a white towel on the marble slabs; she motioned for us to lay face up. A thin veil of humid steam hung in the air between us.

We did not speak. Saida motioned for us to lay still and relax. She returned 30 minutes later and took my hand. She guided me to stand under the running warm shower. When I was done, she brought Hudson over to the shower, too.

Wet and relaxed, we stood in the mist. I felt Saida's hand take mine and she returned me to the marble slab. I watched as she did the same with Hudson.

We had never taken a hammam before, so everything was new. Chakir had said it was like a Turkish bath, but that didn't help, as we had never done that either.

Relaxed and alert, I felt Saida rub oil all over me, rigorously. Her sarong was soaked and stuck to her skin. She was wearing a red mitt on her hand. After the oil rub, she slathered a thick abrasive mixture on my skin, scouring and exfoliating it.

I was struck by how unselfconscious I was about my naked body. Considering how much we show of our bodies back in the states, we are modest in locker rooms and beaches.

After the scrubbing, Saida held my hand and guided me again to the shower. The warm water washed away the exfoliating scrub and my skin felt like soft, smooth and oily.

After Hudson took a shower, we both put on our robes and babouches. I was guided to a massage room and Hudson sat poolside and drank water. My modesty aside, I removed my robe and got up on the massage table. Saida massaged my back, legs and arms for an hour.

When I emerged, Hudson was laying on a chaise next to the indoor pool.

"Can I go swimming now?" he immediately asked, standing and taking off his robe.

"Sure, now you can go skinny dipping," I smiled as he walked down the steps into the pool.

Lying back on a chaise next to Hudson's I watched his naked body swimming through the water. It felt so intimate, as though we were the only ones in the hammam.

I ran my hands down my arms, surprised at how smooth they felt.

The experience at the hammam was intimate and required full trust. It was among the most intimate not sexual, experiences I have ever had in my life.

Traveler's Tip:

In Morocco, the Czech Republic and France, we visited the capital cities. Two hours outside each of those cities were emotional, exhilarating and sensual experiences.

Advice: get away from the urban environment and off the beaten path. See and experience other ways of living.

Morocco: Marrakech to Essaouira = 2 hours

France: Paris to Bayeux/Normandy Beaches = 2 hours

Czech Republic: Prague to Český Krumlov = 2 hours

A first-time tourist to the United States would include New York City as part of their visit. Two hours north is Branford, Connecticut. A lovely shoreline town, Branford is representative of New England with culture, recreation and that pace that allows a newcomer to feel a place.

We know. We live in Branford.

Chapter 6

Germany

Three world maps hang in our home. Two Rand McNally maps illustrate country borders in six colors. Often I sit at my desk and stare at the world and wonder, what are the other seven billion people doing right now? Much has changed in the world since I was young. But my love of studying maps, looking at them long and hard, has been consistent.

The third map, tacked to the wall of Hudson's bedroom, is from Luckies of London. It is a scratch-off map and is one color — gold. The map was designed to scratch off countries visited. It hangs next to Hudson's bunk bed. Using a penny, he removed the gold outer layer to reveal blue for Canada and the United States, acid green for France, Germany, Austria, Hungary and the Czech Republic. When we returned from northwest Africa, Hudson rubbed the penny across Morocco to expose ochre. The penny sits on the corner of Hudson's desk, awaiting its next task on the map.

"Where are we going next year?" Hudson asked, as we sat in the plane on the runway in Casablanca.

He had tears in his eyes, and so did I. Morocco was a wonderfully warm and kind country.

Looking at my son, I said "First, let's know how lucky we are to be able to ask that question, ok?"

He nodded.

"Let's go to every continent, mom!" Hudson suggested.

"Love it! We've seen North America, Europe and Africa so far. Where to next?"

Back in Connecticut, we took our brainstorming ideas to John Weinstein at Adler Travel. We talked about traveling to Asia or South America, possibly even Antarctica, the continents we had not seen yet.

John had great insights and wisdom. The timing, we reminded him, was limited to the North American summer months, after school ended. So we looked at dates from late June to mid-August.

"Typhoon season in Asia is during our summer months," he advised. "It's winter in South America and Australia during our summer. Have you ever thought about Central Europe?"

"What is considered Central Europe?" I said.

"Countries that were previously called Eastern Europe," John answered.

Hudson and I looked at each other. We were open to suggestions.

John continued. "How about Germany, Austria, the Czech Republic, and Hungary?"

Leaving his office with Central Europe brochures, we talked about making those four countries our next destination. When we got home we went online and looked at maps and read about Berlin, Vienna, Prague and Budapest. The more we read, the more excited we got about visiting those four capitals.

We are flexible when considering new places to travel. We both love to learn and enjoy a sense of history. Differences pique our curiosity, not our fear. It was decided. Central Europe was our next adventure!

June 29, 2012, Hudson and I landed in Berlin's Tegel airport, day one of our two-week tour of Central Europe. I have to retrain myself to say Central Europe instead of eastern Europe.

"They are re-marketing themselves in that region, and 'Eastern

Europe' is perceived as severe. Plus it sounds Communistic," John had explained.

When we checked into the Mercure Hotel in downtown Berlin, we were told our room wasn't ready. The front desk clerk took our bags and suggested a walk up the strasse to Checkpoint Charlie, the name given by the Western Allies to the Berlin Wall crossing between East and West Berlin during the Cold War.

Construction site walls along the sidewalk told the history of the neighborhood, Germany, and the world. The black-and-white photographs depicted a black-and-white time in history. The actual checkpoint was now a kitschy makeshift booth. It featured an enlarged image of an American soldier on one side and a Russian soldier on the other.

Vendors at tables set up on the sidewalk, sold remnants of the wall, t-shirts, pins and other WWII memorabilia. Although it was somewhat tacky and exploitive, we acted like tourists hovering over the tables.

"Mom, can I buy this t-shirt?" Hudson asked, holding up a red shirt. The words on the front of the shirt were taken from the famous border sign: You are leaving the American sector, written in English, Russian, French and German. He bought two military pins as well. He paid the vendor, and walked away with his first souvenir of the trip.

While eating pizza at an outdoor café on Friedestrasse, Hudson spotted a store he wanted to go in that sold sunglasses.

"Germans have the coolest sunglasses," he said, pointing to the store across the street. "Can I get a pair?"

We walked over and he quickly found a pair he liked and bought them. The pale yellow lens of the sunglasses reminded me of Bono, the lead singer of U2, sans angst.

Jet lag had grabbed ahold of us. We walked back to the Mercure hotel. The room was ready; we took the elevator up and settled in. The carpeted room was actually a suite. Two rooms, one with a king-sized bed, overlooked a construction site with an active crane.

In the adjoining room was a sofa, desk and TV. Both rooms were brightly colored shades of red and green and blue, colors that reminded me of IKEA, or children's playscapes.

Once showered, we put on pajamas and slept from 5pm to midnight. When we have traveled in the past, we try to adjust to local time, but sometimes succumb to what our bodies are saying. In this case, we were exhausted and just went to sleep. We woke up at midnight and played our favorite card game, War. Hudson has been a history buff since he was in elementary school and was aware of the history of war in Berlin.

"Isn't it funny to be playing War in this city?" Hudson joked.

The next morning, we dressed and went downstairs to the breakfast buffet in the hotel. It featured hams, cheeses, eggs, some frankfurter-like food we couldn't name and potato pancakes. The food was different than we would see in the United States, offering more lunch-type meats.

Two things continually strike me while dining in Europe. One is the quieter speaking tone, a low murmur of voices. The second is the small size of the coffee cups.

Over breakfast we talked quietly, lowering our American volume, deciding to visit the Reichstag first. A German parliament building, the Reichstag was built in 1894 and destroyed by a fire in 1933. Reconstructed between 1958 and 1972, it became the center of German government. When the Berlin wall fell in 1989, the capital moved from Bonn to Berlin.

Berlin, with a population of 3.5 million people, is the most populous city in Germany, a country of 82 million residents. We noted the population of Berlin and Connecticut was similar.

We waited in line for an hour. When we reached the front, we were asked if we wanted to go into the Reichstag now or later.

"Now, please," I answered.

With order and efficiency, we were directed to another queue to show our passports. Our names were put on the tour list for 13:00, military time. Many people in our assigned tour group took advantage of the outdoor seats at a nearby café. We stood by and watched a group of performing artists manipulate a life-sized, yellow jointed puppet. We saw many street performers while we were in Berlin, but the six adults who harmonized their movements to simulate a walking puppet were the most adept and talented.

Then we were instructed to gather and cross to the Reichstag together as a group. At the top of the stairs we entered a glass vestibule and filed into the parliament building. We were led to the key architectural feature that had been added by UK architect, Sir Norman Foster. Like the I.M. Pei addition to the Louvre, the glass dome atop the Reichstag was criticized at first. And like the addition to the Louvre, it was a complete departure from the original building.

Two things struck me about Berlin. One was the efficiency — there was consistent, serious precision about time and action. We observed this at the airport, the hotel, and even the Reichstag tour. The communication was clear and precise; events started on time.

The second was the lack of trash. There was no garbage and no garbage cans. Where were all the cigarette butts? It seemed we were the only ones not smoking.

Apparently Berlin has a buzzing night life, too. Prior to our trip, we had read a lot about Berlin, and every article and guidebook mentioned the lively night scene. I can't comment on this as Hudson was only twelve years old at the time, and I didn't have a sense of the night scene. Dinner was our night scene.

Once within the Reichstag, we were directed to a long, high desk. Cassettes and ear pieces were distributed in several languages. With precision and efficiency, we were guided to the glass top. The cassette recording directed our attention to details of the city of Berlin. So much of Berlin's history was influenced by World War II. I found it inspiring that the people of this city had rebuilt and rebranded it.

After completing the tour, we walked outside and sat on the steps to talk about what we wanted to see and do next. The Brandenburg Gate was around the corner and an obvious choice. While walking there, we spotted an outdoor café with small tables with white table cloths and wooden chairs. We sat at a table and looked around at the plates on the other tables for ideas. The apple strudel with vanilla ice cream seemed popular and looked delicious, and touristy enough for our first taste of German pastry. After scraping the plates clean, we left our euro on the table and walked to the square.

Like the Arc de Triomphe in Paris and Washington Square Arch in Manhattan, the Brandenburg Gate in Berlin served as an architectural landmark, commissioned in the late 1700s by King Wilhelm II. Its twelve Doric columns and neoclassical arch were designed to represent peace, and later victory.

Brandenburg Gate anchors the Pariser Platz, the lively cobblestoned pedestrian zone and touristy square. Embassies stood in the background and street performers filled the area. Gigantic human-sized bubbles were blown by a man with a wand while horse-drawn carriages clomped past. In this car-free zone, segways, rickshaws, and even a circular bicycle rolled by us. The bicycle driver pedaled while seven tourists sat in a circle holding handlebars.

Two street performers dressed in World War II military garb lured tourists from a small rectangular wooden stage. Two young men, one dressed as an American serviceman and the other outfitted in German army gear, were holding the flags representing their countries. They dramatically posed with the Brandenburg Gate as their backdrop.

Hudson and I watched for a while, enjoying their antics. We paid them three euros and got on stage with them. We were handed army hats and instructed to salute. A photographer, part of the act, took our picture. We were quintessential tourists.

Our peacetime picture in hand, Hudson and I thanked the performers and walked towards the sound of music. Three men and a boombox were set up on the cobblestones. Their exaggerated and satirical dance, to the music of the movie Titanic, included gymnastics and hip hop moves. One dancer in a white t-shirt extended his arms and leaned dramatically toward the audience. His partner kneeled beside him and grabbed the bottom back of his shirt. He ruffled it to look like wind blowing. We nodded and laughed, recognizing the "I'm flying" scene from Titanic. They were good and they knew it. The third performer passed a porkpie hat and collected donations.

We joined the crowd in our applause, then walked away, seeking shade. One constant companion in Central Europe was the heat.

With the Brandenburg Gate at our backs, we walked without direction or intention. We stopped in the shade and pulled out the Berlin map. We decided being near water would help us cool off.

Seeing Checkpoint Charlie, the Reichstag, and the Brandenburg Gate were on our tourist list of things to do, but taking a boat ride through Berlin was not. One thing I have learned as a mother and a traveler is to leave room for the unexpected, the spontaneous. In Berlin, it meant finding water. How to get to the Spree River?

We studied the map looking for cross streets, then spotted a German guard standing in front of an embassy gate. At this time, the only German words we knew were basic phrases. We showed the guard our map, pointing to the Spree River. He directed us to cross Dorothene Strasse. A few blocks later we were looking at the Spree.

In most of the cities we have visited, English is spoken. When it is not, we keep a cheat sheet of common phrases, like please and thank you, excuse me, where is, and how much. This has helped us throughout our travels as we attempt to connect using the native language. Hudson masters accents and languages quickly.

Looking at the dark, flowing waters of the Spree River, Hudson suggested, "Let's go for a boat ride." We purchased two tickets for a fifty-minute boat tour, then stayed inside on the wooden boat to cool off, drinking Coca-Colas.

As we passed significant land sites, an unseen tour guide spoke over a loud speaker. The guide spoke in German, French and then English, highlighting details and features. We passed parks, residential areas and the Reichstag.

After the tour, we disembarked and walked along Friedrichstrasse. Shops and outdoor cafés lined this main road. Hudson pointed out that every café table had an ashtray and no salt and pepper, the opposite of at home.

Back in the hotel, we cooled off, played War (I lost) and washed up for dinner. Our last night in Berlin, we ate wiener schnitzel at an outdoor café. We were the only table not smoking.

After checking out the following morning, we took a cab to the Berlin HBF train station. We found our way to Rail Europe train #173 headed southeast for Prague.

CHAPTER 7

The Czech Republic

Prague

We had purchased Rail Europe train tickets online a month before our trip. The Berlin Hauptbahnhof or HBF station was easy to get to, modern, immaculate, and simple to navigate. The large LED screen overhead displayed track information, and we made our way to train #173. We said goodbye to Berlin and Germany and departed for Prague at 8:45 a.m.

The coach train was crowded with seats configured in groups of four. Hudson got out the deck of cards and we played War (again) and I lost (again). Once outside Berlin, the ride southeast to Prague was quiet and rural with occasional forests.

We arrived in Praha, as the locals call it, at 1:15 p.m. into Praha hlavní nádraží, a gorgeous, expansive, glass-ceilinged train station. We pulled our luggage off the top shelf. Our first stop was the exchange counter.

New country, new currency, and I loved this exchange rate (especially compared to the euro) of $1 = 18.3 Czech korunas. Money is fascinating to study. Who are those people on the bills? There were different size bills for different denominations. Even the coins, substantial and heavy, were interesting. Our money musing aside, we walked out front to hail a taxi. No need to hail, there was one right outside the door.

The brusque driver propelled us at breakneck speed to the Century Old Town Hotel, giving us our first glimpse of Prague. A departure from Berlin in many ways, the city has a third of the population of Berlin, so it felt more intimate. Clean and modern, Berlin had felt crisp. Prague felt gritty, old-world, almost medieval in comparison. Most notably, Prague was untouched by both World Wars; the 9th century architecture was the reminder. For more than forty years, communism governed Prague. Evidence of those four decades is apparent in the architecture.

After checking into the hotel, we were advised to wheel our luggage down the hall to the elevator. Like many in Europe, the elevator was tiny. I thought of the corny joke about the room being so small you have to go outside to change your mind.

Off the elevator, we walked down the hallway looking for our room. The corridor walls were decorated with countless black-and-white photographs of Franz Kafka and his wife. Hudson said her nickname should be "horse teeth." I laughed in agreement.

I felt less self-conscious there. Prague felt earthier than Berlin, and not pretentious. Since we arrived the temperatures had been very high, even by July norms. Berlin had been in the upper 90s, and the heat wave followed us throughout Central Europe. I resigned myself to sweating and went without makeup.

I match Prague better. Its gritty, romantic, tight streets were freed from communism in 1989. The city has soul and warmth, old world charm, and an active river scene.

Every so often, I would slip and say, Czechoslovakia. We referred to Rick Steves, author of our travel guide, for the facts: "The nation of Czechoslovakia — formed after World War I and dominated by the USSR after World War II — split on January 1, 1993, into two separate nations: the Czech Republic (Česká Republika) and

Slovakia." We later learned that the Czech Republic was more industrialized, while Slovakia was agriculturally focused.

The tracks of an electric cable car were steps from the front door of the hotel. The hotel clerk gave us walking directions to follow the tracks toward the Old Town Square. We walked briskly, as we needed to be on time. We wanted to get to the square before the top of the hour to experience the Astronomical Clock.

Crafted more than 500 years ago, the clock chimes hourly. The tour book had told us about its details. The timepiece offers a 15th century worldview on time and prejudices. It is adorned by three symbols: The first, a lazy Turkish man plays the mandolin, symbolizing hedonism. The second, a Jewish banker or moneylender, represents greed, and the third, a nationless man, looks into a mirror, representing vanity.

On the hour, Death tips the hourglass and rings the bell. Two blue doors then open, allowing the 12 disciples to parade. A rooster crows to end the show. Death mocks life.

The Astronomical Clock does more than tell time. It shows the location of the sun and moon and identifies the current zodiac sign. It is ornate and colorful. We learned it is one of the three oldest astronomical clocks in existence.

I considered the concept of time. I used to view it as something I did not have enough of. I know better now. I feel less reactionary and rushed. I will always be Hudson's mother, though, and I know my time with him is limited. In 2017, he'll graduate from high school and has plans for college and beyond. He will belong to the world soon enough.

The clock show ended and the crowd dispersed. We slowly walked to the Charles Bridge. Seventeen bridges cross the Vltava River; the Charles Bridge is the most famous.

The Vltava River splits Prague down the middle. We were on the east side where the Jewish Quarter, New Town and Old Town are located. The Charles Bridge crosses the Vltava to the Castle Quarter and Little Quarter, otherwise known as the Lesser Town.

It was hot and crowded as we made our way slowly to the bridge entrance. We passed tiny shops selling t-shirts, jewelry and postcards, Russian dolls, and other tourist items. Packs of people from Asia stopped frequently for group shots. They posed dramatically in front of statues, church steps, and the river.

Blackened sandstone pillars mark the entrance of the Old Town Bridge, built in 1357. Local artists lined the sides of the open span. They sold paintings, drawings, jewelry and caricatures drawn on the spot. Entertainers and singers added to the lively, festive atmosphere. Only foot traffic is allowed on the 679-yard (one-third mile) bridge. We zig-zagged our way across, passing thirty statues of various saints, placed on the bridge between 1683 and 1714.

There was a queue at the statue of John of Nepomuk. His defining feature was a crown of five gold stars. Other tourists instructed us to put our right foot on the gold spot on the ground and our five fingers on the stars at the base of the statue.

"Make five wishes," they said.

Just five?! My wishes included staying healthy, finding my life purpose, showing daily gratitude, clarity, and being able to continue to travel the world with Hudson.

Hudson stepped up and silently made his five wishes. It was the first of many legends, stories, and superstitions that added to the charm and mystery of Prague.

Sometimes I stand back and look at my life, and marvel where it has taken me. From small town Brookfield, Connecticut to college in upstate New York, a journalism stint in Atlanta, ten years in New York City, a marriage and a son. I feel blessed, proud and lucky to have a son who loves to learn and travel as I do.

Christian statues and iconography were everywhere in Prague. They decorated every corner and bridge, and were featured in store windows. The abundance of religious icons was especially interesting, as seventy percent of modern Czechs consider themselves atheist.

Each statue or relief we passed had a spot to rub for luck. It was obvious where to rub, as the area was well worn and often a completely different color than the rest of the statue.

Charles IV was the king responsible for building the bridge, as well as the first university in Northern Europe. He was fascinated with numerology. His fascination fascinated me. According to legend or history, or a mixture of both, Charles laid the bridge's first foundation stone on July 9, 1357 at 5:31 a.m. Written out, it creates a numerical palindrome: 135797531.

We looked over the side of the crowded bridge at the sandy Vltava River flowing beneath us. Tourists filled rowboats and paddle boats as they explored Prague from the water.

We meandered across the bridge to arrive in the "Lesser Town." This section of Prague was called lesser because it sat lower on the river. We descended a wide flight of grey stone steps and found ourselves level with the water. Multiple river excursion signs advertised seeing the city from the Vltava. A paddle-wheel boat tour was boarding and we took advantage of the schedule. A recorded tour guide surprised all onboard with a fact: Prague has more bridges than Venice and Amsterdam. We drank Coca-Colas and enjoyed the respite from the heat.

From the boat, we counted sixteen arches on the Charles Bridge. Concrete V's were constructed before the arches. We later learned they were ice guards, placed to crush and break up ice floating downstream. It was hard to imagine ice on that relentlessly hot day.

After the fifty-minute boat tour, we disembarked. We strolled back over the bridge. Hudson bought refrigerator magnets that featured images of the Prague castle and Charles Bridge.

As we walked through Old Town, Hudson said, "A lot of people travel with their dogs here." There were many dogs and they accompany their owners into the shops. We saw a charming alcove with trellises covered in vines. A cobblestone walkway lead hungry tourists to an open-air restaurant. Outdoor seating with picnic tables was framed by trees. Tied to one of the picnic tables was a well-behaved medium-brown dog whose breed we couldn't name.

We studied the menu and decided to share chicken for two. I asked the friendly waiter about the goulash, and he brought us over a taste sampler of thick brown stew with two pieces of bread for us to dip into it. I ordered a Pilsner Urquell 12°. When the waiter returned and asked how our meal was, I said, "This is the best beer I have ever had."

Julie, my longtime friend, was arriving the next day from London. She had never been to Prague before either, and we were excited to discover someplace new together. Julie is a petite, brown-haired old soul, with quiet presence and strength. She is one of the best listeners I know. She has an ability to stay focused with extended conversations and reserve judgment. We worked together selling leather — while I sold to architects and interior designers in Manhattan, she did the same in London. I have shared my soul with Julie and have always felt her unconditional love and respect.

We had agreed before the trip to set up a walking tour with a native guide. When Julie arrived, we had two hours before our guide arrived.

Hudson and I took Julie to see the Astronomical Clock.

"We have the time," we joked.

Off to the clock and back in time to meet with Andrea Reznickova, the native Prague city tour guide. Tall, attractive, earthy and well-spoken, Andrea was knowledgeable and proud of her heritage. She asked us a series of questions about what we wanted out of the tour, and what we knew of Prague and the Czech Republic.

We all agreed we wanted to learn as much as we could about Prague and the Czech Republic. But we also wanted to hear her personal stories about what life was like there.

Hudson added, "I need to find a church in Prague for my Russian teacher."

I've mentioned before that Hudson had been studying Russian privately since the seventh grade. When he told his Russian teacher, Daria, that we were headed for Central Europe and Prague, she asked Hudson to do some research for her. Could we find the Russian

Orthodox Church where her grandmother Olga and grandfather were married?

She gave Hudson a copy of a black-and-white photograph of her grandparents walking out of the church on their wedding day, with no date. She thought the photo was taken sometime in the early 1930s.

He explained his special project to Andrea and she outlined the tour around getting us to the Saints Cyril and Methodius Russian Orthodox Church on Resslova Street.

She included Hudson in all the questions, unlike some adults who ignore children and defer to adults. She was fantastic, the perfect ambassador for Prague and her native country.

"I am the typical Czech. I am proud, slightly sarcastic, and an atheist, and I love beer," she offered, smiling warmly.

As she walked us through the Old Town square, she pointed out sites. Occasionally she stopped us to just take in a panoramic view of what was around us.

"Do you see that building with the plaque on it?" she asked.

We all nodded. It was about twenty yards away.

"That plaque has a relief of Albert Einstein on it. That's where he used to teach," she said.

She walked alongside us and took us to the Charles Bridge. She repeated the palindrome numerology story.

Hudson was wearing his cool Berlin sunglasses when he was suddenly approached by a Filipino man.

"Superstar! Superstar!" the man said, smiling. He asked Hudson to get in the picture with him and his family.

Picture taken, we laughed and continued over the Charles Bridge. Andrea mixed tourist information and personal knowledge as she recounted what life was like in Prague for her parents during communism.

"They are always urging me to buy stuff," she says, "because for so long they couldn't."

It was an interesting commentary on consumerism. Julie offered comments on materialism in the United Kingdom and we offered parallel insights from the United States. Our stories intersected. We talked about our cultural similarities — we'd all grown up with values and cultures that endorsed amassing stuff. Our throw-away capitalistic countries endorse, support, and promote buying even if there is no need.

We ended our time with Andrea at Café Louvre at Narodni 22, an ornate café with endless gorgeous pastries. It has impressive history as well. Franz Kafka and Albert Einstein used to eat and drink there. My strawberry sangria arrived with a straw and I quietly and happily drank as Andrea discussed the itinerary for the next day. Hudson scooped the whipped cream off his hot chocolate with a spoon. We agreed to meet at nine the next morning for a three-hour walking tour. Andrea told us we would start in the Jewish Quarter and end at the base of the castle.

With our plans set, Andrea said good-bye. Julie, Hudson, and I walked along Narodni Avenue looking for a place for supper.

We smiled as we saw the gold ring and elephant on the side of a building. Andrea had walked us past this site earlier. She pointed them out and explained they were good landmarks in the neighborhood. We sat outside and ate Italian food. As we walked back to the hotel, thunder and lightning threatened. We made it back to the hotel just as the rain started.

We said goodnight to Julie, then Hudson and I headed for the third floor. We took showers, fell into our respective twin beds, and were asleep within minutes.

Our hotel stay included breakfast. We met Julie at the buffet on the first floor after passing images of Franz Kafka and "Horse Teeth." The expansive buffet included meats, cheeses, breads and jams, eggs and fruit and coffee and juices. After breakfast we sat in the hotel lobby waiting for Andrea. We were looking forward to another day of learning.

"Ready to go to the Jewish section and tour the synagogue?" she asked upon arrival.

The Jewish section was small and well-preserved. Andrea told us that the Old-New Synagogue was the oldest landmark in Jewish Town, and was one of the oldest surviving synagogues in Europe.

We took a few steps down into the entry of the synagogue. Hudson was handed a yamaka and instructed to keep it on during the tour. He placed the blue and white yamaka on his head and we silently walked through the 13th century structure. The interior, monastic and severe, was divided by gender. Women sat in the back, separate from the men.

I feel huge in this space. I moved slowly and thoughtfully, looking at the Hebrew inscriptions etched onto the walls. The handout translated the eight biblical verses and inscriptions. There were verses from Ecclesiastes, Berachot (two), Zechariah, and four Psalms.

I wrote my three favorites down in my travel journal:

"I place God in front of me always." (Psalm 16:8)

"God is one and His name one." (Zechariah 14:9)

"Shun evil and do good." (Psalm 34:15)

All the verses strike me as words of wisdom applying to people, not just the Jewish people.

When we exited, we took a few steps and stopped while Hudson took off the yamaka. I put it in my messenger bag as a memento of the visit.

As we walked, Andrea stopped frequently to point out various styles of architecture that were found in Prague. At one turn, she handed us each a timeline of architectural types. Images of Prague buildings representative of each style included ten types of architecture: Romanesque, Gothic, Renaissance, Baroque + Rococo, Classicism, Revivalist (Neo Renaissance), Art Nouveau, Cubism, Social Realism and Post Modern. The buildings date from 800 AD through present day.

We left the Jewish Quarter for the Charles Bridge (Gothic architecture style) crossing to the Lesser Town to a café.

"I want to take you to a place where I go with my friends," Andrea explained, "so you can see Prague from a local point of view."

We walked quietly for a while. Suddenly, Hudson yelled out and pointed, "Mom, look! A schipperke!"

We walked faster towards the man with the schipperke on a leash. When we reached him, we asked, "schipperke?"

Hudson quickly added, "Spitz?"

The man nodded. It was clear he did not speak English. The spitz or schipperke had frizzy, puffed fur, unlike our schipperke, Chase. With unspoken gesturing, the man indicated it was ok, to pet his dog. Hudson and I felt immediately sentimental for our dog back in Connecticut.

For the most part, English was spoken throughout Prague. This was one exception.

Led by Andrea, we shuffled through the Lesser Town. Not a tourist in sight. We stopped for lunch at a café that had chalkboard paint walls and wide plank floors. Gazing at the menu, Hudson asked, "Mom, can I have the shrimp pasta?"

I nodded, "Sure. Go for it."

Hudson has an openness to food and new experiences. This attitude makes it easy to travel with him. He's not a picky eater and he likes to try new food. The shrimp pasta arrived, an adult portion, and Hudson ate it all.

Hudson ate, Julie drank tea, and Andrea and I sipped on cappuccinos. We settled our bill with Andrea. We owed her 1800 koruna for six hours of time. An excellent use of our time with a warm and knowledgeable guide. I felt this was a real value. Thanking and hugging her, we promised to return and to recommend her to everyone we knew.

From there, the three of us went vertical, toward the Prague castle. It's visible from everywhere in the city, sitting high on a hill overlooking the Vltava River.

Built in the 9th century, it is the world's largest medieval castle and the home of the president of the Czech Republic. Representing all the architectural styles from the last 1000 years, the castle includes four churches and four palaces, three halls, and eight towers, houses and residences. It is surrounded by eight gardens. Beautiful and commanding by day, it was magnificent at night, aglow in gold hues. It gave the city of Prague a romantic backdrop.

An hour into our walking ascent on cobblestone streets and stairways, the castle in sight, we spotted an outdoor café with three tables. Julie and I were hungry and Hudson needed a drink. After eating and drinking, the waiter came by and asked us, "Are you ready for the check in Czech?"

Probably not the first time he'd used that line.

The remaining walk up the cobblestone street to the castle was quiet. We stopped twice to catch our breath. When we arrived at the top, we toured St. Vitus Cathedral (Gothic architecture style, my handy timeline showed),

From the city below, St. Vitus Cathedral is the most dominant sight within the castle walls. Historically, it has been the location of services, coronations, and burials. The Gothic cathedral is dramatic, with flying buttresses that look like stone lace. Ornate stained glass windows colorfully offset the grey stone.

Two soldiers stood at the exit on either side of the archway, positioned in vertical coffin-like structures. We steadily observed them to confirm they were real. They were. They were costumed in sky blue polyester uniforms that were neither the right color nor the right fiber (polyester is not comfortable in high heat) .

Satisfied with our aesthetic judgment, we walked away and stood admiring the panoramic view of Prague. We opted to descend through the vineyard, cutting through rows and rows of ripening grapes. Occasionally we stopped to make a comment or just take in the whole of Prague.

"What a great city," we all said at different times.

Off the terraced castle hill, we walked to a store selling tram tickets and bought three. Andrea had given us instructions on where to buy tickets and which stop to get off. We boarded the tram. It ran on tracks and was electrified, and crowded. Finding no seats, we held onto the straps overhead.

Our stop was the Cathedral of the Little Jesus. We walked up the steps to enter the tiny cathedral. It was obvious where the little Jesus was encased — he was surrounded by a crowd.

Little Jesus, a tiny statue doll, was dressed in a burgundy ermine robe with white lace detailing. He wore a crown. He was ornately decorated and white. The three of us looked at each other, knowing this was not the time or place to have an opinion. Silently, we exited. On the steps outside we agreed that the Jesus we knew of didn't wear an ermine robe and crown. We preferred the hippie version of Jesus.

Next stop: The Dancing House — the nickname given to the Nationale-Nederlanden building — and Hudson's research project.

We walked toward the Russian Orthodox Church, just up the street from the Dancing House. The postmodern building was designed by architects Frank Gehry and Vlado Milunić. The Dancing House appeared as two buildings was actually one. Two distinctly different shiny silver facades met in the middle. One half appeared perfectly straight, while the other leaned in. The windows undulated, giving the appearance of movement. In a neighborhood and city full of Baroque, Gothic and Art Nouveau, this deconstructivist or "new Baroque" style stood out. It had been built to look like Fred and Ginger dancing, as one writer suggested, "Czech to Czech."

Hudson was motivated to provide his Russian teacher, Daria, with photos and details of the church where her grandparents were married. With just a photo copy of the church in his hands, Hudson studied the details of the exterior. Some features matched.

The church was within sight of the Dancing House. We walked up the street to its entrance. The doors were locked. Around the corner, the crypt door was unlocked. We all walked in. Hudson was looking forward to putting his Russian fluency to work. He spoke Russian to the man behind the counter. The man seemed cranky. He corrected Hudson and said the church was no longer Russian Orthodox, it was Czech.

Handing Hudson a business card, he said the dean of the cathedral could answer his investigative questions. He turned his back to us; it was clear he had nothing more to share. We looked at each other and silently exited. The Soviets had occupied Czechoslovakia for many harsh years, and many Czech people still resented this. We felt this in his hostile exchange. The cathedral itself was not open, so Hudson took many exterior shots of the building to bring back to Connecticut for Daria.

By tram and by foot, we journeyed back to the hotel. The concierge recommended a restaurant within walking distance. She urged us to order the special appetizer. We took her advice and were delighted when a warm pretzel, the size of a dinner plate, was served.

Over dinner, the three of us talked about what we had seen — the Charles Bridge, Astronomical Clock, and castle were the highlights. We promised to see each other again soon. We all agreed Prague was fascinating and worth another visit in the future.

The next morning, we said goodbye to Prague and to Julie. As she left for the airport to catch her flight home to London, Hudson and I got in a small white car bound for Český Krumlov. Leaving the capital city for a small hamlet, we were excited to see what the rural countryside was like.

With a population of 15,000, Český Krumlov in the southern Czech Republic was within miles of the Austrian border. The driver, a non-English speaking man, made one more stop to pick up two more passengers, a couple. The woman sat in the front passenger seat and did not speak the entire journey. The man sat next to Hudson in the back seat and occasionally looked over and smiled at us.

On the 113-mile ride south through unspoiled countryside, Hudson and I played hangman. We got increasingly sillier as the trip progressed.

Český Krumlov

Two and half hours later, we arrived to the sounds of screaming. "What's going on?" Hudson asked.

The driver parked in front of the Hotel Gold, took our suitcases out and placed them on the gravel roadway. We thanked him. He silently nodded and was gone.

Screams and sounds of a gushing waterfall compelled us to walk to the bank of the Vltava River, the same river we crossed countless times in Prague. The river was wide and muddy. Occasional rocky lengths created white water. The screams, happy and fun, were coming from people on kayaks, rubber rafts, and canoes. They navigated the river with varying speed and risk.

"I want to do that!" Hudson exclaimed. "Let's go!"

I hesitated, thinking we needed to check in, unpack our bags and settle in, maybe re-read what Rick Steves had to say about visiting Český Krumlov. Then I snapped out of it, realizing we only had 36 hours there. I was excited to do something spontaneous, adventurous, and fun.

The Hotel Gold was a simple two-story plaster building. Painted a pale mint green, it was decorated with white details and molding. It felt sweet, like a confection. It had an open-air patio as entryway, white walls, arched doorways, and an immaculate slate floor. We wheeled our suitcase to the front desk.

A petite woman greeted us, asked for our names in English, and checked us in. We were given a key to the room with instructions to return the key to the front desk when going out, a common request in Europe. I was happy to oblige as the key was attached to a chunky, heavy brass fob the size of my fist.

The hotel was cozy and felt like a guest house. Our ground floor room was just off the entryway atrium. With whitewater rafting on our minds, we left our bags in the room, unopened, and headed right back out the door.

Determined, we walked into town to find the place to rent a

rubber raft. Conveniently located on the bank of the river was a rental company. We entered and talked with a young man who introduced us to a guide, Janya. "Just call me Jane," she said when we hesitated to repeat her name. She told us the details and fitted us for life preservers. She drove us up the river to the company's warehouse. Once we got there, a man brought a bright yellow rubber raft and three life jackets to us. We were handed oars. We carried the raft to the bank of the shallow murky Vltava River, and set off!

Riding white water rapids on that hot sunny early July day, we saw Český Krumlov (translated, it means Czech bend in the river) from the river first. It is a fairy-tale village with narrow cobbled streets and wooden bridges. The Vltava River wraps the town in a tight lasso.

Oars in hand, Hudson and as I sat on opposite sides of the raft. Janya sat in the back and acted as guide, rudder, and cheerleader. With rocks ahead, the river swirled white, and Janya instructed us to "keep paddling!" After the rush of white water, the river calmed. I got the camera out and took pictures of the buildings reflected on the water. We disembarked downriver an hour later, feeling exuberant and hungry.

We thanked and said goodbye (děkuji a nashledanou) to Janya and asked her for a recommendation for something to eat. She suggested walking to the castle and snacking along the way.

Like Prague, Český Krumlov has a castle that sits high up, overlooking the river. We had seen the hamlet from the river and now we wanted a higher vantage point. As we made our way along the cobbled, hilly streets, we read signs directing visitors to the castle. All streets lead up to the castle.

Castles have defining features and characteristics. Though they are romantic today, the first medieval castles were constructed as fortified structures. The design of all castles was defensive in nature and intended to guard and to protect the owner. Most castles have a moat or a ditch surrounding the property; a keep or tower; a bailey, where the rest of the household lived; a curtain or defensive wall and a gatehouse. The Český Krumlov castle has a unique feature, the cloak bridge. And this is what we ascended to see.

The smell of sugar and cinnamon caught our attention. We stopped along the way at a miniscule bakery where Hudson ordered a sugar-covered "bracelet," a hefty doughnut smothered in cinnamon and big enough to slide onto his wrist. He did just that with his sugary treat and nibbled at it until it was about to fall off. I took a bite and ordered one for myself. Hot, sugary, and dense, the doughnut bracelets were devoured.

With every turn, we could see the castle with dark grey and brown stones, gateways. The white, red, and blue Czech flag flapped at the top of a spire.

A fan of snail mail and lover of unique cards, I continue to send Christmas cards every year. For the past two years, Hudson and I had selected a photo from our travels and crafted it into a seasonal message. From France, it was images of stained glass and a cross from the Notre-Dame cathedral, offering a message of peace. From Morocco, we used the photo of goats in trees with Hudson perched on a low-lying branch and me standing beneath the tree holding a baby goat with a tongue-in-cheek message, 'location is decoration.'

The view from the three-storied cloak bridge was panoramic and picturesque. The bridge, with its massive stone pillars, was constructed in 1764. Spanning the moat, the cloak bridge was named for its overhead covering.

We stood on the walkway connecting the castle to the Baroque Theater. We said very few words as we took in the sweeping views of Český Krumlov. Within the castle walls were arched cutouts in the stone for wartime artillery. As Hudson took out the camera, he said, "This will be our Christmas card picture." The shot, taken through the arched stone cutout, framed the quaint village below. We wrote, "It takes a village. Thank you for being a part of ours."

Tucked in an alcove was a tiny shop selling only postcards and maps. I bought one with an image of the village. It was pre-stamped.

Since 1983, I have had a pen pal named Bob. Unlike most pen

pals who live half a world away, Bob lives in Brookfield, forty-six miles west of me. We have exchanged cards and letters for three decades. The one postcard I bought in Český Krumlov was for Bob. It was sold with the stamp already on it. I found it challenging to select one best representing the picturesque village.

Like a piece of ribbon candy, the Vltava River was a dominant part of the landscape. No matter where we walked, and we walked everywhere, we could smell and hear water. Foot bridges connected the landscape and there were cozy nooks everywhere. A tourist center, Český Krumlov maintained an authentic charm.

My pithy postcard message written, Hudson and I looked for a mailbox. The bright orange metallic square box was mounted against the side of a building.

I probed every part of the orange box and couldn't seem to figure out how to open it to insert my postcard. After several embarrassing moments and movements, a Czech man appeared and showed me how to open the door to insert the postcard. Hudson walked ahead of me, shaking his head at my ineptitude.

We found a tiny restaurant with outdoor seating. Across the street was the voskove figuriny, the wax museum. I ordered a local, light, white fish of the day and Hudson had a chicken entrée with corn flake crust.

On our last night in the Czech Republic, we ate dinner while looking at an image of Michael Jackson. His wax image was featured on the advertisement for the museum. I thought about the impact and far reach of American influence. Even here, in remote Český Krumlov, we were reminded of our pop culture. It wasn't a political leader or writer or poet or great inventor that was pictured. It was an entertainer.

Though we watched a lot of people walk past our table, we didn't hear any American accents. A lot of dogs and tattoos walked past.

As we finished our dinner, I felt joy. Joy for life. Joy for the love of travel and learning. And most of all, joy for the love of my time with my son.

Above: Me, 4th grade, age 9
Below: Me, age 8, with my Mom and two brothers in NJ

Above: Mom with singer Tom Jones, her favorite performer
Below: Hudson in front of Niagara Falls

Above: Hudson looks for WWII shrapnel on Omaha Beach
Below: Soldiers face home at Normandy American Cemetery

Above: Mont St. Michel at dusk
Below: Goats suspended on the branches of the argan tree

Above: The Bridge of Tolerance at the entrance to Essaouira
Below: Spice market in Marrakech, Morocco

Above: Berlin's Spree River, seen from the roof of the Reichstag
Below: Detail of the astronomical clock in Prague

Above: Quiet moment while whitewater rafting in Český Krumlov
Below: View from our boat on the Danube River in Austria

Above: Cooling off in front of Austrian Parliament building

Above: Me as E.T. in the Blue Mosque, Istanbul
Below: Hudson inside the Hagia Sophia

Above: Hudson attaching our prayers to the wall in Meryemana.
Below: The words "Merhaba, Ya Sehri, Ramazan" welcome Ramadan

Above: Apfelstrudel (apple strudel) at Tucher Am Tor café in Berlin
Below: Hudson eats goulash and bowl in Prague

Above: Homemade vegetarian lunch in Gobeller
Below: Hudson's favorite puzzle of the map of the world

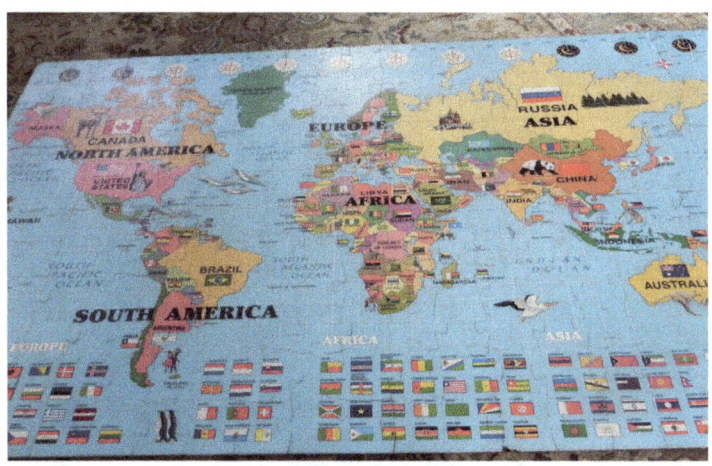

CHAPTER 8

Austria

Vienna

As we waited to depart the Gold Hotel, I wished we had an extra day in Český Krumlov. We had seen Berlin and Prague, and now we were on to Vienna. Though I love urban hum, the pace and quaint size of this tiny Czech town had a cathartic effect on me.

Sometimes I feel sentimental when we transition between places. Leaving Český Krumlov, I felt nostalgic. A Seals and Crofts song came to mind. The words have stayed with me. Seals and Crofts released "We May Never Pass This Way Again" in 1973, when I was 11 years old.

While we sat waiting for the next leg of our trip to begin, I looked at Hudson. Thinking about the words to that song and the meaning, I felt like we lived that song. I was happy we went white water rafting. As much as we both loved Český Krumlov, we may never pass that way again.

Thoughtfully, I wheeled our suitcase to the back of the white van. We had an early morning start. Picked up by a driver and his assistant, Hudson and I were the only two passengers in the back of the 10-person van. The 103-mile ride to Vienna was three hours.

Český Krumlov was fifteen miles from the Austrian border. Crossing into Austria, we saw an unmanned, abandoned check point. It seemed like there should be more fanfare — after all, we were entering another country, with a new language, culture and currency. It was as easy as crossing from Connecticut into New York State.

We were driving southeast, and the ride was lush, green and rural. The paved road was windy and bumpy and we saw very few cars. The road signs previously written in Czech were now in German.

It was soon evident we'd made a mistake sitting in the back of the van. We both felt carsick before we were out of the Czech Republic. Hudson was wilting, hands sweaty and eyes heavy.

"Can you pull over for a minute?" I asked the driver.

Pulling the van over, he asked if we were ok. I told him we were a little sick. He suggested getting some air and sitting closer to the front.

We stepped outside, took deep breaths, and stretched. Hudson walked around the van a few times. He felt better. I felt a sharp pain on my feet and looked down to discover I was standing in the middle of a well-populated red ant colony. I stamped around to get the biting ants off me, which served to distract me from the carsickness. The heat stayed with us. We began to state the temperature in Celsius, as it made us feel better. 34 degrees Celsius sounded cooler than 93 degrees Fahrenheit.

An air of elegance and refinement were my first impressions of Vienna. We checked into the Hotel Rathauspark. Built in 1882, it was once a palace located in the Austrian government district. We were directed by the concierge to visit the Parliament building while our room was prepared.

We left our suitcases at the hotel and walked towards the Rathausplatz, the city hall square. A Gothic government building was the backdrop to the public space where events and festivals take place.

Before long, we were dripping in sweat. Approaching the

Rathausplatz, we saw white tents, food huts and stands. A movie screen was set up against a cathedral. Signs indicated an international film festival was setting up.

We heard a pssst sound and smelled water and felt a whisper of mist on our skin. Hudson and I looked at each other under clear blue skies. "Did you feel that?" I asked him.

Hudson nodded and we both looked around.

"Look there," he said and pointed to a white lamp about eight feet tall. "That lamp is releasing mist, let's go stand under it," Hudson suggested. We stood under the mist lamp, enjoying the dewy refreshing spritz of cool water on our sunbaked skin.

The international film festival seating area was surrounded by food huts offering cuisine from around the world. Hudson loves Chinese food and spotted a vendor selling dumplings.

"We come to Austria, sit at a film festival, and eat dumplings," Hudson noted, eating six Chinese dumplings in the spray mist. Still hungry, he went back to the stand and bought six more dumplings. This struck us both as funny. Our first meal in Vienna was not classic Austrian, but Chinese.

In many cities we have visited, we see and feel the smallness of the world. Chinese food in Vienna, the Russian dolls for sale in Prague, the pizza in Berlin, and the ubiquitous Coca-Cola vending machines everywhere.

I found myself saying, 'like a wedding cake' often in Vienna, as a description of the buildings. The exteriors were ornate, perfect and immaculate.

Leaving the Rathausplatz mist, we walked along the Ringstrasse, or the ring road. A circular pedestrian and motorway built to replace city walls, the Ringstrasse forms a tight five-kilometer (3 mile) loop, creating an inner Vienna. Generous public spaces were marked by pristine green parks. Monuments to Mozart, Strauss and Beethoven were among the many statues we saw.

The ring was a great way for us to get a feel for Vienna. Museums, parks and monuments sat grandly along the linden tree-lined boulevard. Red-roofed electric trams hummed by.

There were reminders of classical music everywhere. Billboards, monuments, signs showcased concerts or exhibits. Home to more than 100 museums, Vienna felt like a museum itself, with a constant call to look back.

The heat was wearing on us and we needed an indoor activity. We walked further to the Museum Quartier, the site of former imperial stables. Art museums and contemporary exhibit spaces were designed as a complex. Before we entered the Leopold Museum, Hudson spotted a tourist shop. We went in and he bought refrigerator magnets with images of the Hapsburg palace and the Danube River, along with two World War II pins.

Hudson said the best thing about the Leopold Museum was the air conditioning, definitely not the Gustav Klimt exhibit. He had suffered art museums with me before and his prevailing attitude was disdain. He prefers realism in art.

Using the museum café as an opportunity to procrastinate before going back out into the heat, we sat and sipped on cold drinks and read from Rick Steves' Eastern Europe travel guide.

Throughout the guide, one family's name stands out above all others — the Hapsburgs, whose empire influenced the city for almost 700 years. The downfall of their European prominence was due to their inbreeding.

"The best spouse for a Hapsburg is another Hapsburg," we learned.

Hudson has had a passion for history since he was very young. His voracious reading has informed his opinions and understanding of the world. He connected the extinction of the Hapsburgs to inbreeding. There are many times when I talk with Hudson that I am the student and he is the teacher. This was one of those times.

Fortified for the time, we decided to see three prominent Viennese sites. The iconic silhouette of St. Stephen's Cathedral with its Gothic spires is to Vienna what the Empire State Building is to Manhattan, and the Eiffel Tower to Paris. It was visible throughout the city, and we used it as our compass.

The predominant language of Austria is German. Hudson knew a little German, and had practiced speaking it while we were in Berlin. He could speak enough to make us seem polite. He was able to communicate well enough to get us to St. Stephen's Cathedral.

The cathedral was closed when we arrived. We were not disappointed. We have adopted a c'est la vie attitude when we travel. The guide book had displayed stunning interior images, and that would suffice. We stood back and admired the roof. From the ground, the 230,000 glazed yellow, grey, green and black tiles looked like intricate embroidery. The roof was so steep, it appeared vertical. Snow never sticks to it, we had read. On the south side, a series of zigzag patterns framed a double-headed eagle, the symbol of the Hapsburg Empire. Equally ornate, the north side revealed a coat of arms.

Our photos taken, we needed a plan B. Blistering heat was taking its toll on us. The dense city center seemed even hotter, as there was no breeze. "Mom was cranky" was not how I wanted Hudson to remember Vienna. We needed water. But before we set off for the Danube River, there was an eclectic monument we wished to see.

St. Stephen's Cathedral was connected to the Graben, a street with Old Roman origins. Now a bustling pedestrian walkway, it is lined with exclusive shops and restaurants. At one time it was a moat for a Roman military camp — graben means ditch in German. It was one of the first pedestrian walkways in Europe. In the middle of all this history and commercialism was an eccentric column.

When the bubonic plague hit Vienna, one third of the population was wiped out. King Leopold prayed for the plague to lift. He promised if it did, he would construct a mercy column as a thank you. The Pestsaule, or plague column, sits in the middle of the Graben. The sculpture, built in 1679, features angels, clouds, Father, Son and Holy Ghost at the top. The monument told the story of the plague, the prayers and of King Leopold's gratitude.

It was fascinating to study. What Hudson and I most wanted to see was the depiction of King Leopold. The Hapsburgs' inbreeding resulted in an exaggerated underbite on King Leopold. He was easy to spot.

Later, when we returned home, Hudson researched the bubonic plague, believing it was a medieval disease. We were startled to discover it was still afflicting people on four continents: North and South America, Asia, and Africa.

The Pestsaule distracted us from the sweltering heat. Exploring the Danube River was next on our See and Do list. Hudson and I had talked about going on a boat tour. Using his polite German, he was able to get us directions to the famous river. We purchased tickets for a one-hour cruise, joining 30 others onboard. Most of us stood outside along the railing to take advantage of the breeze.

The Danube River moves gracefully through nine countries. The river flows east, covering more than 1,785 miles. Despite the title, The Blue Danube Waltz by Johann Strauss, the river was brown and murky. The name means to flow.

An older boat, booths of tables and chairs were set against oversized windows. The boat launched and we fixed our eyes on the green lush riverbanks.

We went inside to purchase a drink for me and an ice cream for Hudson. As we sat eating and drinking, I looked around the room. A woman in a wheelchair was positioned at the bow. Two men stood on either side of her. One man kept looking over at Hudson and me. Every time I looked over at them, he was looking back. Instead of looking away, I held his gaze. Eventually he walked over, smiled and sat with us at the table. What was going on? Austrian flirting? Did he think he knew us?

He leaned in with his tan face and blue eyes. I mirrored his actions, leaning in, ready to listen. He asked a question in German.

I was surprised. The first German words that came to mind were weiner schnitzel, spaetzel, streudel, and gesundheit. Shaking my head, I said, "No, ich spreche kein Deutsch." And then, "I am American, do you speak English?"

Now it was his turn to look surprised.

"American?" he asked.

Tilting his head a bit, he looked skeptical. I wasn't sure if I felt flattered or insulted.

He shook his head, "no English."

He seemed like he had something to say to me.

I offered, "Parlez-vous français?"

Immediately, I realized my college French was long faded. All I would be able to relay were numbers, a few months of the year, my name is, and I love you, none of which would get me very far. A few more random words came to mind that, if spoken, would make me sound more psychotic than intelligent.

He held up his hand extending his pointer and thumb fingers an inch apart, and said, "un peu." (A little)

I smiled and nodded, "un peu."

We had a few moments of awkward hand gestures. He pointed to the people he was with and I indicated Hudson was with me. We politely smiled at each other quietly, understanding that this was as far as the conversation could go. He stood up and nodded, shook my hand, and walked back to the people he came with.

I never did figure out what he needed to say. But that virtually wordless interchange impacted me. After a few moments of introspection, I came to a conclusion and made a decision.

I concluded that it was arrogant of me to come out into the world and assume the world spoke English. And I decided I needed to take action. When we returned home, I was going to learn French — really learn it, so I could communicate with more people in the world.

I signed up for a French 101 course that fall. I have graduated beyond counting and the months of the year and am capable of talking with someone as long as it is in the present tense. I can confirm what all the studies claim: It is harder to learn a language when you are older. But only un peu.

Thank you, unnamed Austrian man with blue eyes, for expanding my language skills.

A loud clap of thunder cracked, signaling the end of the boat tour. Hard, heavy rain poured down. We ran off the dock and were instantly drenched. Looking for quick cover, we stood under a nearby tram waiting area. Hudson and I huddled under the overhead eave.

Hudson had read about a museum that he wanted to see, so we looked at the tram map and figured out how to get to the Heeresgeschichtliches Museum. The Austrian military museum, as we called it, was a short walk from the D tram, which we rode for 2.4 euro.

Austrian war history, photos and equipment. One hundred percent real, just the way Hudson preferred museums to be.

Modern-day Austria borders eight other countries. Much of the museum's artifacts and documents displayed how difficult it was to establish and maintain borders in post-WWI Europe.

We stepped outside to view army tanks, lined in a row. Hudson rested his arm against the caterpillar tracks.

We exited the museum three hours later, saturated in Austrian history. Just as I was about to suggest a means of transportation back to the ring, a hop-on, hop-off tour bus pulled in.

"Let's get on that bus, mom," Hudson suggested.

We approached the front door and asked the driver if he spoke English. He nodded. We inquired about the cost and route, paid and sat down and put on a set of headphones to listen to the guided tour. Clean, crowded and air-conditioned, it was a great value.

I stuck with the English version, while Hudson experimented with the other languages offered on the headset.

"Mom, the Portuguese version talks the longest," he told me.

Hudson has been attracted to other languages since he was seven years old. In the 2nd grade, he used his birthday money and bought a picture book of German phrases and commonly used words. Soon after, I bought him a German CD. He would put on headphones and repeat phrases in German. His accent was remarkably authentic.

He began studying Russian in the seventh grade, through Aux

Trois Pommes, a private language center. His interest extended beyond the language to include Russian history, culture and literature. He proudly counts War and Peace among the books he has read.

Berlin and Vienna are two immaculate, perfect, efficient cities. Prague and Český Krumlov are sandwiched between them, and the after-effects of communism are visible and palpable. The Czech Republic felt grittier, more soulful and vulnerable.

As for my Citizen of the World, he and I departed Vienna from the Westbahnof train station on the 9:54 a.m. Rail Jet to Keleti Station in Budapest. Next stop: Hungary.

"So far, whitewater rafting in Český Krumlov has been my favorite thing on this trip, mom."

"Me too."

CHAPTER 9

Hungary

Budapest

From Westbahnof station in Vienna, we boarded Rail Jet to Keleti station in Budapest. For three hours we ambled along countryside dotted with windmills. With a constant whirring and humming, the windmills looked as if they were waving to us on the train.

We sat quietly for long periods of time, just looking out the window. We were weary and the gentle rocking of the train had a calming effect on us.

Hudson was thrilled when the attendant pushing the food and drink service cart on the train appeared. He ordered a Coke and I had a coffee. It took his mind off the family of four who sat diagonally across from us. Observing them since we boarded, he commented frequently and decisively about their blasé attitude and embarrassing American-ness.

Since our first international trip to France in July of 2010, Hudson has prided himself (and me) on the fact that many people don't know we are Americans. Americans are stereotyped as loud, large, entitled and pushy, and lacking in sophistication.

Hudson commented about the young American boy and girl,

whose singular concern was their electronics. When they first sat down, Hudson noted, the first thing they did was pull out a pile of wires and charging devices.

"Mom, those kids don't even appreciate the train ride and haven't looked out the window once," he said. I, too, started to observe them. The husband and wife sniping answers with disdain and the two kids — they were younger than Hudson, who was twelve on this trip — each absorbed in their respective handheld devices. I felt dissatisfaction from all four of them.

I started to think about Americans. All of us. What happens when everything has been done for you? What do you strive for? Is it natural to turn back into yourself and become selfish and self-absorbed? Does coddling create a different kind of need?

This family seemed affluent and unhappy. Next to their mound of wires and adaptors and chargers were boxes, wrappers, and remnants of their lunch.

Up until this point, we had not seen many Americans. I felt a paradox. Their mannerisms, look and energy were familiar, but we were on a train from Austria to Hungary. It was the same feeling I have had when I see someone out of context, not in their usual habitat.

They were outwardly attractive, but their communication with each other was limited, clipped, and angry. They were unaware of the scenery, the windmills, and the transition from Austria into Hungary. They were focused on their electronics and food. What were they missing?

Outside the train, forests and hills rolled by. We passed the occasional town, with a church steeple, a cluster of buildings and a few people. We saw a glimmering, rocky river ramble by for a few moments. The sights outside were bucolic and did not distinctly say "Central Europe."

I wanted to be distracted by the outside, a book, my thoughts, but I kept observing the American family. What was I watching them for?

At one point, the husband starting talking with a woman who sat behind him. To his fortune, she was a native Hungarian who spoke English, and offered insider insights on Budapest. The wife and two kids did not engage, even when the husband attempted to share some of the local woman's suggestions and wisdom.

Pausing after witnessing their lack of intimacy and joy, I silently thanked that family for showing me the abundance in my life. My interest in observing them faded. I felt sad. I understood why Hudson liked it when people could not identify us as Americans.

We are lucky and we know it. We are blessed to have the discretionary income, time, interest, and guts to go out in the world. We go out in wide-eyed wonder and everything is fascinating.

"First world problems," Hudson said taking out the deck of cards and dealing, getting ready to play War.

Yes. First world problems. When every need is met, that is when it is time to turn outward — to service. Help other people get their needs met to keep life in balance.

As Hudson dealt the cards, I thought about raising a citizen of the world. What are my goals for him beyond food and shelter? He is a white American boy. What is his American Dream? As his mother, I want him to have a worldview. I want him to be aware of others and to lift his eyes up beyond Connecticut and the United States. Every headline reminds us of our global economy. We are all connected. I also want him to be humble and be thankful for all that he has been born into.

Aside from awareness of the world — the big picture — I want him to have empathy for the struggles of others. The attitude of "if it's not happening to me, it doesn't matter" does not serve the greater whole.

There is a lot being written and said about narcissism. Aside from being excessively surface-driven and selfish, narcissists are apathetic and do not care about other people. Many writers have suggested we live in the age of narcissism, the age of "Me."

Experiencing, not just reading about, other cultures is one way to offset the prevailing narcissistic culture we live in. Traveling to real places, not synthetic ones such as Disney or Las Vegas, is another way to cultivate openness.

Separate from the journal notebook Hudson and I keep when we travel, I keep a small black notebook. In it are inspiring quotes, bits of advice, conversation highlights, and book title recommendations.

As we travel, I am reminded of one of my favorite quotes: "It's not what you look at, it's what you see."

Here are two facts we did not know before going to Hungary: The first is that Budapest is actually two cities. Buda and Pest are split down the middle by the Danube River. Our hotel, the Zara, was on the Pest side.

The second is that Budapest is synonymous with thermal water. There is a thermal cave system under the surface of the city, with more than 123 hot-water springs. Those springs are the source of healing hot water to more than two dozen thermal baths. We decided before we left home that going to a thermal spa in Budapest was a top priority. Experiencing the Széchenyi thermal spa was our first adventure in Hungary.

Exchanging euros and dollars into Hungarian forints ($1 = 200 HUF) required a focused mind. Suddenly the bills seemed huge. So when we caught a cab from the Keleti train station and it cost 4000 HUF, Hudson was quick to remind me to calm down. It was only $20.

Budapest was the last city on our two-week tour of Central Europe. It was our fourth capital city. And like Prague, it had lifted itself from more than 40 years of communism.

It was hard not to make comparisons, as each city we visited had its own distinct personality. One surprise connected the four countries and five cities: Water.

During the planning stages of this trip, we had talked about visiting historical sites (Reichstag, Charles Bridge, Český Krumlov castle, museums of Vienna, and the Széchenyi baths) with the exception of visiting the thermal baths of Budapest. We had not talked about swimming, or about water at all. And yet every city we visited, water played a big part of our experience.

In Berlin, we took a boat cruise down the Spree. We saw another side of Prague from the Vltava River, where under the Charles Bridge, we learned about the castle written about by Franz Kafka. Later, in Český Krumlov, we went whitewater rafting down that same river — the Vltava, in what was the single most spontaneous event of this trip. In an effort to get relief from the 36° Celsius heat in Vienna, we toured the Danube River. And in Budapest, we walked to the chain bridge that crosses the Danube, connecting Pest to Buda. The water highlight in Budapest was the day at the Széchenyi thermal baths.

Our anticipation was high as we checked into the Zara Hotel on Dohany Street. We weren't sure what traditional Hungarian design looked like. This hotel lobby felt more Turkish, with mosaics and archways and smoky gold and brown colors. It felt sophisticated, with a welcoming, modern vibe.

We checked in and took the elevator to our room, small and cozy with two double beds.

"Mom! Even the toilets are different in Hungary!" Hudson exclaimed from the bathroom. "Come and see!"

He was right. And it was a first for me, too. There was a square toilet.

We dug out our bathing suits and got ready for the thermal spas so widely celebrated in Budapest. We spoke with the concierge about going to a thermal spa. We mentioned Széchenyi, and he told us that was where the locals go. He showed us a brochure of the Gellert spa, an alternative "that some tourists prefer."

"We want something authentic," I said to him.

He advised us to stick with our first choice, Széchenyi. We bought all-day tickets for 3800 HUF ($19) each. He advised renting a locker for our things. We told him we wanted to walk, but he suggested taking a cab because of the heat and the confusing layout of Budapest.

Unfolding a map of the city, he circled our current location on

Dohany Utca (street) and the Széchenyi fürdő (spa).

"The cab ride will be fast and cheap, and much cooler than walking," he assured us.

It would also save us from figuring out the map. As much as both Hudson and I love a good map, we were ready to do something immediately.

The bath was built in 1881, first built on the Pest side of Budapest. With its mustard-yellow exterior, the Széchenyi spa arched and curved around the street. It looked and felt old-world.

The taxi dropped us off in front of the baths. We could see masses of people inside the entrance door.

We approached the check-in counter. Handing the clerk our receipt from the hotel, we were given purple wrist bands and directed to keep them on all day. We rented a cabin, a 4' x 4' room, where we immediately changed into our bathing suits. We left our clothes and shoes in the room. The room locked behind us. The purple wrist band was the way to reenter.

Taking it all in, we meandered outside. Three pools, each with different levels of activity and movement, were full with people of all ages, nationalities, and sizes. The two-story spa building was a golden yellow with three bright sky blue pools reflecting the sun.

"Let's go in the hot one first," Hudson suggested. Walking over to the 100° F pool, we passed a warning sign advising us not to stay in for more than 20 minutes.

We slowly stepped down the stairs, passing two men playing chess by the side of the pool. As hot as it was outside, the pool water felt soothing and relaxing. The water height was consistent, hitting my upper chest. There was almost no movement in the pool. The intent was to relax and rejuvenate.

As cautioned, we exited after 20 minutes. Dripping wet, we made our way through the crowd to the center lap pool. Significantly cooler, it shocked us when we first dipped our toes.

Suddenly, we heard a sharp whistle. We looked up. The lifeguard was whistling and pointing at us! What were we doing wrong?

Pointing at his head, he indicated we needed to wear shower caps.

We stepped out and reentered the building to find a shower cap. We were told they were 100 HUF (50 cents) and where to purchase one.

Thinking we would share it, we purchased one shower cap. There was one size and it was enormous. If we could manage swimming like Siamese twins both our heads could have easily fit into the shower cap.

Back at the lap pool, Hudson put the shower cap on. It covered his head, face and part of his neck. He adjusted it to sit on just his head. With the first jump in, the cap came off and floated away in another direction. I sat on the pool steps watching and laughing. Although he made several attempts to refashion the giant shower cap to stay on, his efforts were futile.

We didn't know it yet, but the most fun was ahead. There was a reason the next pool was the most crowded. Spontaneous underwater spouts pushed water from the floor up, like an underwater eruption.

When the underwater spouts stopped, people milled about the pool. Then suddenly the eruption would draw people towards the propulsion. You could tell which areas of their bodies ached, as people leaned into the jet to relieve back aches or hung their arms over for an upper body massage.

We needed to be alert and quick. When they erupted, people of all ages zipped towards the geysers fast and furious.

Stealthily we waited. Hudson pointed to a small gurgle at the bottom of the pool. We lurched toward to the eruption. Got it! Leaning back, we let the jet hold us up. It was relaxing and fun. Plus, the 86° water temperature was perfect.

While leaning back on the gurgling spout, Hudson pointed over to a part of the pool where people were screaming and laughing.

"What's going on over there?" he asked.

"I don't know, let's go find out," I answered, giving up my coveted spout spot to an older woman.

We shuffled across the crowded pool and came upon a short brick wall. It was a pool within a pool.

We stepped onto the edge of the pool and made our way toward the fun. The pool within a pool was shaped like a capital letter C with a smaller letter c within. The squeals, laughter and shouts were the sounds of pure delight.

Hudson and I entered the current; we joined in the flow of fun. The smaller c was a seated hot tub. Around the hot tub, a strong current of water pushed all who entered. The force of the water launched us right into the person in front of us.

Causing a domino effect, each person would gush into the person in front of them and a peal of laughter would come from everyone.

People let go. It didn't matter what you looked like, your age, how much money you had, or your country of origin. There was no divisiveness, no competition. What bubbled out was spontaneous delight. We heard several languages in that pool — some we recognized, others not. Laughter was the universal language.

The day in the Széchenyi pools is tattooed on my memory and heart. It was ideal, the setting and the people, the way it could be if we could find our similarities in laughter and see what is common in people as opposed to what is different.

We took a cab from the spa back to the hotel. Mellow and calm, we walked through the crowded hotel lobby. We showered and got ready to walk around the city.

We walked to the chain bridge, looking at the Buda side. When it was completed in 1849, the chain bridge was the second-longest suspension bridge in the world. Built of cast iron and stone, the bridge crosses the Danube River connecting Buda to Pest. It was named for the long lengths of chain that connect the roadway to the pillars.

Looking down into the Danube River, we watched the murky brown water amble east. We walked onto the pedestrian walkway on the chain bridge for a better view of the two cities and the river. The heat was getting to us and we decided to walk back to pick up some paprika. We had read about Hungarian paprika and wanted to bring some back home for ourselves and some friends and family.

We walked through a group of vendors and heard the Beatles "Let it Be" playing in the background. We went into a shop near the vendor bazaar and asked for real Hungarian paprika. The employee smiled and directed us to a display of Kalocsai paprika. Festive red, green and white packaging identified the three degrees of spiciness. We bought four packages.

Hudson suggested taking the hop-on, hop-off bus back to the hotel. We hoped it would be air-conditioned like the one in Vienna. When an open-air bus pulled up, we took our seats amongst the other sweaty, red-faced tourists drinking water and taking pictures.

After the seventh stop, we got off. Hudson spotted a Turkish restaurant. Eating falafels and drinking Cokes, we decided to spend the balance of the day and night on the hotel rooftop. Swimming in a pool overlooking Budapest at night would be the perfect ending to our day.

There were two rooftop pools. One indoor, for laps, and the other outdoors, for relaxing. We swam for four hours. Hudson broke his underwater handstand time record of 25 seconds.

It was our last night in Budapest and on vacation. We ate at a refined Hungarian restaurant, Rezkakas. A band of four men was playing "Lara's Theme" from Dr. Zhivago when we arrived at 7pm. We had no regrets or disappointment in not seeing the Buda half of Budapest. "Next time," we said to each other.

Sharing a bowl of goulash soup and chicken with paprika, Hudson and I reviewed our summer 2012 journey. We recapped highpoints from each place we visited; the Reichstag in Berlin, the boat ride on the Danube in Vienna, the walking tour in Prague, white water rafting in Český Krumlov, and the day at the Széchenyi spa.

We talked about our previous trips to France and Morocco and agreed how lucky we were to be able to see the world, meet new people… and return home.

Chapter 10

Turkey

Istanbul

"Inshallah," the airport employee said, walking back to the crisis center in the Ataturk International airport in Istanbul.

Right. Inshallah. I had forgotten about Inshallah, the phrase we had heard so often in Morocco. It means "God willing" in Arabic, and it had ended so many conversations we had there. It was the last word I wrote in my travel journal, too.

A stark contrast to the last words I heard at JFK airport in NY as I waited outside the men's room for Hudson.

"Pull up your pants!"

An airport employee, in a navy blue skirt and gold name tag in the shape of wings, hissed at a young African-American man. His tan pants were cinched by a black leather belt at his upper thigh, exposing baby blue boxer shorts.

Her hissing startled me. I watched them to see what would happen next. Noticing me as her audience, she continued.

"He's walking around in his underwear, like that's okay," she stated, shaking her head. I nodded, bobbing my head and smirking in agreement.

Inshallah.

When we arrived in Istanbul after a three-hour delay at JFK, we discovered Hudson's suitcase missed the flight. An annoying beginning. Our two choices were to wait in the airport three more hours until the next New York flight arrived in hopes it was carrying his luggage, or go to the hotel, meet up with our tour group and wait for it to be brought over later.

We opted to wait in the airport. We were cranky, tired and hopeful for the next flight. Our tour was scheduled to leave early the next morning, and we were concerned the bag would not catch up with us in time.

We tried to remain positive. Were the delays in New York and Istanbul signs that we should not have come to Turkey at this time?

Protesters had filled Taksim Square and Gezi Park for the past six weeks. Unhappy with the directives of Prime Minister Erdogan, who had been in power for ten years, they took their dissatisfaction to the streets. The protesters showed up nightly in downtown Istanbul, demanding his resignation. They were looking for a secular republic and his politics had gotten increasingly more Islamic-oriented.

Before we left home, Hudson and I received texts, phone calls and emails from friends and family voicing varying degrees of concern and anxiety about our going to Turkey. I did waffle, and we did craft a Plan B (Argentina), but in the end we prevailed and stuck with our original plans. Turkey for two weeks.

Every life situation can be approached with optimism or pessimism. The glass is always half full for me. This attitude has sustained me. In the Istanbul airport, hearing "Inshallah" kept my optimism alive.

With a transatlantic flight behind us, we had been traveling for twenty-four hours straight. Exhaustion and exasperation were taking hold of us. In the airport that Friday afternoon, three men redeemed my faith in humanity.

When there are snafus in life, and there always are, I have learned to adopt a new attitude. Perhaps it is a coping mechanism. Either way, it works to keep me calm and give me perspective. I ask myself one question: "What am I supposed to learn here and now?" Many times the answer is patience.

A Maya Angelou quote taped on the wall of my home office came to mind:

> *Seek patience*
> *And passion*
> *In equal amounts.*
> *Patience alone*
> *Will not build the temple.*
> *Passion alone will destroy its walls.*

The three men at the Istanbul airport all connected to me and Hudson, in an honest way.

The first, a father traveling with his wife and three children from JFK. He spoke Turkish, and upon our arrival he kept us informed of the suitcase debacle. We kept our eyes on him, and when he moved to carousel three to wait for his lost suitcases, so did we.

The second was a Turkish man who handled the disgruntled travelers and answered all questions about lost luggage. He took us through the process as we waited to file our lost luggage claim and later advised us to wait for the next flight.

"Is our luggage on that flight for sure?" I asked.

"Inshallah," he replied calmly.

Unrelated to lost luggage, a Russian man with a warm smile and kind face approached and asked if the carousel we were standing in front of was for the flight from Moscow.

"I'm not sure. We are here waiting for the flight from New York," I said. "Are you from Russia?"

"I am. I live in Turkey now. I am waiting for my son to arrive from Moscow," he answered.

"We are from the U.S. My son is studying Russian," I said, indicating Hudson.

"You do?!" he said excitedly to Hudson, and said a few words in

Russian to him.

Hudson politely answered in Russian, adding that he was a beginner.

The man told us he was going to see if his son had arrived and walked toward the luggage carousel.

We watched for a while, as the airport was relatively quiet and we had nothing else to do but wait. We saw him approach a young man and ardently kiss his head. It touched me, the unbridled affection this man felt and showed to his son.

They walked towards us, knowingly. We were friends. One small interchange and there was a connection. He walked toward us and introduced his son, a handsome young 20-something man.

"This young man is from America and is studying Russian," he told his son in English.

His son turned to Hudson and spoke Russian. I stood by and observed, saying nothing, but feeling so much. Hudson had exhausted his Russian knowledge and the older man turned to me and said, "Do you need help?"

His kindness and genuine appeal affected me. I could feel the authenticity in his question and I felt he would help me if he could. The kindness of strangers always gets to me. I had felt this often in Morocco as well. The connections with people who will gain nothing from their actions. It was selfless and sweet. Does vulnerability allow us to be open to experiences?

"Thank you for offering. We are just waiting for the next flight to bring Hudson's suitcase to us," I said and shook his hand.

They said good-bye and walked away, unlikely realizing how much their presence and ability to connect affected me.

I think about those three men, and that is how I tell the story of our first day in Istanbul. They were stories of connections and kindness, not delays and aggravation. I shared this perspective with Hudson, and he tells the story the same way.

The luggage did come in on the next New York flight. We met our van connection outside the terminal. We were driven to our hotel in a white van with a non-speaking driver. Hudson looked at me and said, "I have to pee."

I spoke to the driver, "excuse me, sir. Is there a place to pull off for a toilet?"

His reflection looked back at me through the rearview mirror. His eyes said, "I have no idea what you just said."

Over his shoulder his hand extended what appeared to be a calculator.

I took it showing it to Hudson who said, "It is a converter, a language converter."

Traveling with a thirteen-year-old in 2013 was wonderful for countless reasons. At that moment, I was most grateful for his technological confidence and expertise.

Using his thumbs, Hudson typed, "My son has to use the WC." I handed the device back to the driver, who read it and nodded into the rearview mirror. Soon after we pulled into a gas station and Hudson ran to the bathroom.

When we got back into the van, we nodded and smiled our thanks to the driver. He never spoke, but nodded back. It was non-verbal communication, a universal language of nods, smiles, and gestures.

Arriving after 8 p.m. at the Parksa Hilton in Istanbul, we missed the welcome reception for the tour. Our guide, Gökçe Tascilar, called and filled us in on the details for the next day.

"How do you say your name?" I asked.

"Goke-chay" was her response.

I repeated it. Did I just call her goat cheese? I told her we would be up and ready for the 8 a.m. departure.

Travel to Turkey presented us with three firsts. One: We consciously chose to visit when there was strife. It was not civil war, but unrest. I do not want to be afraid of the world, but see it clearly and unfiltered.

Two: Up to this point, Hudson and I had explored three

continents: North America, Europe, and Africa. Istanbul is the only city in the world that spans two continents. Though we landed in Europe, the majority of this trip was spent in Asia.

Three: We traveled on a tour bus. I'd been long reticent about traveling on tour buses. I have elected to travel autonomously in the past. Encouraged by my travel agent and friends, this time I was persuaded to sign onto a guided tour.

I had a perception about tour travel. It appeared people were shepherded, like cattle or sheep. I wondered about the authenticity of it. I believed tour groups went to tourist places and were told what to eat, think, and feel. I thought it was antiseptic.

But in truth the tour allowed us both independent and group time. We were able to break away and explore our other interests. The other truth, and surprise, was that we liked the people on the tour. We weren't always in a hurry to get away from them. We learned a lot about them, and from them.

Another benefit was having someone else do the navigating and driving. Hudson and I played cards, read, talked, and got to know the other people on the tour. Sometimes we quietly looked at the window and took in the landscape. There were sixteen of us who boarded the bus early Saturday morning — fourteen friends we hadn't met yet.

Our first day in Turkey was spent visiting the most famous sites in the city. Topkapi Palace, built in 1459, was our first experience with Istanbul. For more than 400 years the royal residence was home to sultans. The extensive complex featured gorgeous yellow rose gardens and numerous courtyards and galleries, as well as access to some of the interiors. In one living room or sitting area, mosaics of cobalt blue, yellow, and white complimented the nearby wall, adorned in mother-of-pearl tiles.

The tour guide suggested walking to the furthest point and working our way back. Once there, we sat on a low stone wall overlooking the Bosporus strait. We watched long, heavy tankers, seemingly oversized for the waterway, plod deliberately north and south, while small ferries flitted across east and west.

The Bosporus strait, the watery boundary between Europe and Asia, connects the Black Sea to the north with the Sea of Marmara to the south. A second strait, the Dardanelles, spills into the Aegean and ultimately the Mediterranean.

We couldn't help but talk about Homer's *Odyssey*, one of the books Hudson had read recently in school. The Aegean was right there! We talked about the Topkapi Palace as we wandered through the gardens, and in and out of buildings decorated with bright floral mosaics, low sofas, and arched doorways.

The location was both a beautiful overlook to the strait, as well as the highest point in the city. We stopped occasionally under the shade of trees in the gardens. Hudson consulted our guidebook, sharing facts. By the time the palace construction was complete in 1459, the whole city was being rebuilt.

Hudson read aloud. "Just six years prior, in 1453, Constantinople fell to Mehmet II, the sultan who commissioned the building of the lavish royal residence that would be home to sultans for four more centuries."

It was a powerful start to what would be an inspiring journey through Turkey.

"Once known as Byzantium, Emperor Constantine conquered the city in 324 and renamed it Constantinople. For 1,000 years it was the richest city in Christendom, with the church, Hagia Sophia, its crown jewel. In 1453, Mehmet II, an Ottoman sultan and Muslim, changed the history and religion, and renamed the city Istanbul," he read.

Reviewing the history in our guidebook, we had a question. All the historical images we saw showed the Turkish flag with its red ground and white crescent moon and a five-pointed star. If Islam came to Turkey with Mehmet II in 1453, why did the flag have the symbol of Islam, the crescent moon, on it?

This led us to read further. The moon and the star preceded modern Turkey, symbolizing pagan origins. The red represented warrior blood spilled while serving Turkey.

We met our group back at the designated spot, the tree with the hollowed-out trunk near the entrance gate. As we waited for the others to gather, we introduced ourselves to the couple standing next to us.

Marnie and Geoff were immediately friendly and likeable and made easy conversation.

"We're from the U.S.," I said extending my hand.

"Australia, Melbourne," they answered. "First time to Turkey?"

"Yes, and you?"

"Yes, first time to Turkey. We arrived yesterday from Greece. We took a ferry across from one of the islands."

"Do you travel a lot?" I asked.

"We're retired, so we travel quite a bit now," Marnie answered, listing the many countries, cities and continents they had been to.

They were impressive and inspiring, their stories about their homeland were as well. They had already been to Gallipoli, a WWI site scheduled at the end of our tour, and told us what a powerful place it was to see.

"A lot of history there for ANZACs," Geoff said.

We had read about them, the Australian and New Zealand Army Corps, the ANZACs. Formed in 1915 to fight in the Battle of Gallipoli, they were disbanded a year later.

"It was important for us, as Australians, to see it." He didn't say much more, but we could feel his emotion about the visit there.

That World War I battlefield visit, site of a 1915 fight between Turks and ANZACs, would be on our last day on the tour, and it would prove to be emotional for us as well.

Walking distance from the Topkapi Palace was the Blue Mosque. As we stood in line, our tour guide Gökçe instructed us to remove our shoes before entering the mosque.

"Women will need to cover their heads and shoulders with a scarf or shawl. If you did not bring one, the mosque provides them at the entrance," she advised.

We were handed plastic bags for our shoes. I pulled my white cotton shawl out of my bag. I bought the shawl for our trip to Morocco for the very same reason, to visit the interiors of mosques. I hadn't worn it since then.

At the Hassan II mosque in Morocco, the largest mosque in Morocco and Africa, I had worn the shawl around my waist. I was told my shorts, exposing my knees, needed to be covered.

We were guided into a small space. Much of the interior of the mosque was partitioned off, protected from tourists and non-Muslims. The entire floor area of the mosque was covered in woven Turkish rugs. Each overlapped the next, so we couldn't see the floor.

"It smells like feet, bad breath and B.O. in here," Hudson whispered.

He was right. Those three odors came together and stuck to us, the way cigarette smoke clings to hair and clothes. The interior of the mosque was not air conditioned and was as hot inside as it was out.

The Blue Mosque, or Sultan Ahmet Camii, with its six minarets, was built in the early 1600s. The interior had no furniture. It was empty, except for the thick layered rugs on the floor, and the decorative blue tiles on the ceiling surrounding a chandelier.

"Please, take my picture here," I asked Hudson.

The ceiling tiles were a work of art. Posing for the camera, I instructed Hudson to be sure and capture the ceiling in the frame. More than 20,000 handmade tiles in shades of light blue, turquoise and cobalt adorned the mosque ceiling. The tile theme was simple. All 20,000 tiles featured tulips. There were more than 50 different types of tulips painted on the surface of the tiles.

Tulips originated in Turkey, not Holland. They were widely celebrated as holy symbols, as well as signs of wealth and abundance. In the 16th century, the first seeds and bulbs were brought to Holland from Turkey. No doubt, the people of Holland have done a better job marketing the tulip as their flower.

Hudson snapped the picture. Olga tapped him on the shoulder.

Would he take a picture of her and Ann? Olga and Ann were on the tour with us. They were warm, smart and friendly. Hudson was happy to help them.

Exiting the Blue Mosque, we waited outside for the others in the group to emerge. Hudson took out the camera and leaned in close.

"E.T. phone home," he squeaked, in his best E.T. imitation.

On the camera's display window was the picture he took of me in the mosque, my white shawl draped around my very brown skin, the tulip ceiling in the backdrop. I looked just like E.T.!

Another unknown benefit of traveling with a tour was the guide. Gökçe, a native of Izmir, a city on the west coast, offered a local's opinion and direction. As a group, we lumbered through the streets of Istanbul. She corralled us into a corner away from the crowds.

"The Grand Bazaar is for tourists," Gökçe said. "Turkish people don't shop there; it is the same stuff over and over and over again."

One person, holding up a tourist book as testament, said that it was one of the suggestions for visitors to do.

"Most of the trinkets for sale in the bazaar aren't even made in Turkey. They are made in China. Turkish people do not benefit when you shop there," she explained. "You decide and I will meet you here in two hours."

With that she walked away and disappeared into the throngs of people.

Hudson and I looked at each other. We were tourists, and decided to walk in to see it.

She was right. The arched entrance of the Grand Bazaar was cavernous. Once inside, all the shops were selling the same things. We strolled up and down a few aisles, seeing the same items for sale: t-shirts, rugs and lamps, tea and spices. Boxes of Turkish delights, sugary cubes presented before a meal that are a traditional Turkish hospitality treat, were stacked everywhere. Hudson bought a red t-shirt and we exited past the evil eyes.

Everywhere we looked we saw evil eyes. Evil eyes are sold by vendors throughout the country.

The evil eyes were not from the aggressive vendors. Walking up to us, invading our personal space, they would ask, "Where are you from?"

This was where our anonymity was most useful. With my mid-summer tan, I was as brown as the Turkish people, and many addressed me in Turkish. I shook my head no. I resisted speaking, which would give away my American accent. Hudson's white skin, brown hair and eyes, and slender frame offered no clues as to his country of origin either.

The evil eyes hung in the entrance and windows of most shops. Gökçe later told us, that they do double duty. They are for sale and part of the decoration of the store.

The evil eyes were round tri-çolored pieces of glass with cobalt blue around the exterior, a light blue inner ring and a center dot, or eye of cobalt blue.

Evil eyes hung in the airport, in every doorway both entering and exiting; we saw them embedded into sidewalks, on key chains, hanging off backpacks and handbags, and on billboards. At the end of dinner one night in Istanbul, the waiter handed us the bill along with two evil eyes attached to a blue satin ribbon.

"They keep evil thoughts and words away," Gökçe told us, as she pulled her own evil eye from her bag. This reminded me of what Chakir had said about the hand of Fatima on the doors of Moroccan homes.

Evil eyes were for sale everywhere. I was intrigued by what they stood for. Later on, in Cappadocia, I bought one.

Before she cut us loose in the Grand Bazaar, Gökçe had taken us to Aynen Durum for kebabs. It was a tiny, cramped outdoor grill with people sitting elbow-to-elbow on plastic stools. The smell of barbeque smoke sat heavy in the air.

The kebobs were grilled in front of us. The meat or chicken, when cooked, was shoveled into a thick white disc of bread, which was laid out on a bed of tin foil. The cooking, serving, and delivery were gruff and robust. The place felt like a spontaneous happy eating community gathered on the sidewalk.

A communal plate packed with pickles, peppers and onions was placed in the middle of the table. Messy and delicious, it was one of the tastiest meals we had in Turkey.

We sat amongst Turks, which made me feel we were at an authentic place eating freshly made food. There was not much talking, just reaching for peppers and pickles, smiling at one another.

I felt real joy in that moment. The food was fresh and delicious. The people eating around the grill were unpretentious. And I was with my son. I often pause at moments like that and create a snapshot in my mind. I stayed present, so as to create a visual tattoo. I felt fortunate to have the son I have, and to be able to afford these experiences. He will belong to the world soon enough. I savored lunch and the sentiment.

On our first day in Istanbul, standing at the front of the bus, Gökçe demanded our attention.

"I am going to teach you how to speak Turkish!"

The bus was quiet.

Gökçe was an earthy, hands-on, warm presenter. She had brown hair and eyes and tan skin without makeup. Her hair was pulled tight in a small ponytail. She had a grittiness and zest about her.

"Repeat after me," she said with mock authority.

"Tea — sugar — a — dream," Gökçe said. "Now, say it fast."

Tesekkur ederim.

"You have just said thank you in Turkish!" she said, smiling. "Let's say it again, tea — sugar — a — dream. Now fast: Tesekkur ederim."

Hudson and I repeated the phrase several times, hoping to commit it to memory.

"Please is lutfen," Gökçe continued. "Repeat after me: lutfen."

"Lutfen," we said, with varying degrees of aptitude. I sounded like an American speaking Turkish, while Hudson sounded like a native. He gave me a look that said, "Your accent needs work."

"One more," Gökçe says. "Merhaba is hi or hello. Repeat after me, Mer-ha-ba."

"Merhaba," we repeated, sounding like elementary school children.

When we returned to the hotel, the Hilton Parksa, Hudson and I decided to walk around the neighborhood and get dinner out. In the lobby, we overheard the hotel staff talking with others guests about staying close to the hotel as the police were heading up to Taksim Square and Gezi Park, again.

We walked closer to be part of the conversation. The hotel concierge told the small gathered group that when the tear gas was sprayed last time, it reached the hotel. Some of the guests were affected by it. His advice was to stay at the hotel. He suggested going up to the seventh floor where the open-air roof top restaurant and bar were.

"Enjoy the view of the Bosporus at night," he said. "If the protesting continues, the police block streets off. Getting back to the hotel will be difficult, if not impossible."

Hudson and I listened. We took a step outside and our decision was made for us.

Gendarme or jandarma — police in riot gear — were proceeding up the street toward the square. We observed them for a few minutes. Hudson took a picture.

The scene reminded me of the thought processes I'd gone through deciding whether or not to come to Turkey. Prior to leaving home, I had called the hotel in Istanbul for reassurance and information about their current situation. The person I spoke with compared the events to our Occupy movement. I reminded myself that they were in the hospitality and tourism business. I remember sitting back and thinking, *what if something happens while we're there? What if Turkey overthrows Erdogan, their prime minister, and falls into chaos and civil war?*

Safety, fun, educational, different and authentic top the list of "must haves" when I travel with Hudson. The intent is always the same. We hope to have our minds and hearts opened. But civil war was not on the list of experiences I wanted to have with my son.

I waffled. Friends reminded me of Turkey's neighbors — remember Syria, Iran and Iraq are right there. The whole area could explode.

If Turkey did melt down, and we were there, what was I prepared to do? Studying the world map, I looked at Greece to the west and Europe further northwest. Ultimately, though, we had decided to put our trust in Turkey, and went ahead with the trip.

Back inside, we took the elevator up to the roof lounge. We didn't know it yet, but we had friends to meet there. It was on the rooftop that we got to know Jan and Alan Brady from Australia, two professors whose knowledge of history was inspiring.

Jan and Alan were one of those couples that go together. They looked alike and listened and spoke with great reverence for each other. Behind her glasses, Jan had bright intelligent eyes and blonde, short, straight hair. There was no pretension or decoration about her. Her hunger and interest for learning was so fierce that she was able to overcome knee, back, and heart issues. Throughout Turkey, we watched her as she resiliently climbed stairs and plodded through the crowds, all with an upbeat attitude.

Alan was rugged-looking and an excellent listener. He was the couple's photographer and we often asked him to take pictures of us later, as we continued the tour throughout Turkey.

It has been said that when the student is ready, the teacher appears. Jan the teacher and Hudson the student found each other that night.

Jan took an instant liking to Hudson. He confidently shared his opinions about Columbus being credited with discovering America.

"He didn't discover America," Hudson said firmly. "There were people living there already, they just weren't white."

Jan offered, "Just like the history of Australia. The aborigines were there first."

A friendship was born, another unexpected highlight for tour travel.

After this trip, I shifted my opinions on tour travel. It really was easier for someone else to drive and take us right up to the front door. It was lovely to come back to an air-conditioned bus, and relax and think about our next adventure. Physically, it was easier.

As I've stated earlier, one of my hesitations about going on a tour was the idea of being in a herd, moving with a pack of people who I may or may not want to be with. I hadn't thought about the upside — making new friends. Ten days is a long time to travel with a group. We really got to know a few of our fellow adventurers, and they enhanced our trip.

Jan and Alan were very smart and open. Above all, they were talkers and willing to share their knowledge in a non-superior way. Plus they were from Australia, so we got first-hand information and fun facts about their country and continent.

We compared cultures and details about school. They shared stories of their two sons and we told stories from Connecticut and our past trips.

We met people and made friends with folks from all over the world on that trip. Our common denominator was an interest in learning about Turkey and each other.

We talked with Jan and Alan, Marnie and Geoff, Natalia and Tomas, Olga and Ann, and Vera and Marook. They shared their previous travel stories, as well as tales from their homes. Their tales gave us new places to consider visiting in the future. Our interest in Australia and New Zealand was piqued. Ecuador and Colombia sounded so compelling that they went on our short list, and we consider future plans for a trip to India. This was a highlight and a big pro to going on a tour. Plus we all took turns being each other's photographer.

We traveled with intelligent and worldly people. Speaking to us on the bus, Gökçe would teach us about Turkey from a native's point of view. Often, people on the bus would share how things were done where they lived. It made the stretches between cities more interesting, informative and lively.

Across the Sultanahmet Square was the Hagia Sophia basilica.

The Blue Mosque sat on one end of the square and the Hagia Sophia was at the other, like architectural bookends.

Gökçe took us into the Hagia Sophia. Her introduction and overview of the 1,400 year-old Byzantine building was upstaged by a cat.

We had formed a wide circle around her, listening as she explained the significance of the Hagia Sophia. It was difficult not to be distracted in such a gorgeous historical space with 180-foot ceilings. Gökçe told us that Hagia Sophia meant, "Divine wisdom."

Collectively, we all moved our eyes and attention from Gökçe to the floor. In the center of the circle we had formed sat a preening grey and white cat. As if on cue, we all leaned down to pet and snap pictures of our new furry friend.

"We love our animals in Turkey," Gökçe explained. "They are well tended, fed and cared for, and very docile."

Like the cats in Morocco, feral cats were everywhere in Turkey. They were clean and friendly, especially when we packed leftover bread from breakfast. We saw friendly cats and dogs all over Turkey. The Turkish government funded their spaying and neutering, and their ear tags displayed evidence of that.

Aside from the cat distraction, the Hagia Sophia, the church of holy wisdom, was fascinating for reasons beyond its architectural achievements. The stained glass windows, beautiful in design and color, depicted images of the Virgin Mary holding baby Jesus. As stunning and moving as those windows were, what I found most surprising was the Arabic inscriptions on some of them.

Hagia Sophia, once a Christian church, had been transformed into a mosque. All the earlier décor of Christianity remained. Today it is a museum and architectural monument.

Round disks hung on corners. They complemented the Christian artwork, mosaics, and glass. The disks, hung high with their white backgrounds and black Arabic lettering, displayed the names of Muslim leaders, including Mohammed.

Two religions co-existed peacefully side by side, neither upstaging the other. I thought about this as it related to humans. Why can't we be inclusive? Live and let live. God is not elitist. I felt peaceful when I left.

I thought about anti-Muslim sentiments. Turkey was the second Muslim country Hudson and I had visited, and our experiences with the people and culture were positive and affirming. In my collection of reading materials, I came home with a pamphlet asking "What is Islam?"

I was aware of the negative stereotypes, but I wanted to understand Islam. This free pamphlet outlined the basics of the Islamic belief system. I read this and have borrowed a copy of the Qur'an from a friend. I would like to learn more and understand it.

My views on organized religion are negative. Religion seems to be the product of man and does not promote kindness toward fellow man, but judgment based on beliefs and rules. I feel distanced from the religion I grew up in, and feel like a hypocrite when I step into a Catholic church. I have broken too many of their rules. The exclusion of all female leadership and energy eludes me. I feel no connection to the patriarchal values and rituals.

I have made mistakes. I am human. I value and stand by my decisions not to follow the status quo. I felt the hypocrisy the most when I announced I was getting a divorce. I wasn't following the rules; I was being honest about how I felt. I was done with appearances and surface show.

Throughout Turkey, I found myself reflecting on God and belief. In every city, my eye would look toward the highest point on the horizon and it was always a minaret, the tall slender tower where the call to prayer was said by the muezzin. Though today's Turkey is predominantly Muslim with a secular government, its history is powerfully Christian.

Though I grew up Catholic, my beliefs now are too liberal for that church. Spirituality and what little I understand of Buddhism seem more in line with what I believe. As I have gotten older, I can see and live with paradox more and believe there is a purpose for everything. I learn from everyone I meet and everything I do.

I used to love certainty and, to an extent, still gravitate toward a good plan. Becoming a mother made me more flexible, less self-absorbed, and more aware of the impact seemingly small actions can make on a child. Having Hudson helped me want to be a better person.

Goreme Cappadocia

Evidence of Christianity's mark on Turkey, or Anatolia, was depicted in an outdoor air museum. We traveled into the center of Turkey to Cappadocia. Goreme was home to thirty churches from the ninth century. Carved into the volcanic rocks, the cave churches showcased colored frescoes of scenes from the Old and New Testaments.

Visually astonishing and surreal, formations were created from years of wind and rain erosion. The stalagmite-type peaks had small cutout windows. The Turks call them fairy chimneys. In Goreme, many of the window cutouts had small ladders hanging outside for entry and exit.

From a distance it looked like holes in rocks. Once we ventured inside, we saw and felt the beauty and the artwork. The exterior was plain and unassuming rock; the beauty and creativity were on the inside. It reminded me of Morocco.

We stepped into the rough, primitive church caves. Immediately we felt cooler, away from the sun. The frescoes were in good condition. Reds, yellows and brown tones conveyed religious messages. In one cave, planked floors were placed for even footing and easier walking. It was in that cave we saw two skeletons lying in a shallow grave with a plexiglass covering. What a final resting place. Those caverns felt like living museums.

Anatolia, the region east of Istanbul, was the oldest part of the earth Hudson and I had been through to date. The day in the Cappadocia region helped me understand change. Change is growth, change is evolving, and change is inevitable. And change is life.

Our experience in Morocco was so positive and enjoyable, so truly transformative. Turkey had a similar impact on us. It was a complete departure from anywhere we had ever been before. We had known when we decided on a trip to Turkey that it would allow us to touch another continent, Asia, and take us to the furthest point east that we had ever seen.

Reducing to one word, the experience of two weeks in Turkey had on me, I am surprised by the word that comes to mind: healing. I hadn't realized I needed healing.

Healing was related to my pace of life. The slower the pace, the more I felt. This was true in Morocco, too. At first, slower seemed less efficient, which offended my inner need to get things done. The reality was, the slower I went, the more connected I felt, and the more I intuited. When I go slower, I talk differently with people; I hear better in general. I hear more details. I love details.

When I move slower, feel more, and connect more with people, I heal. The healing comes from depth of feeling where I see a commonality with people. The differences are on the surface.

Turkey taught me about the power of visionary leadership. Ankara is the capital, not Istanbul, as I had previously believed. It was there I learned about the love a country can have for a leader and the power of one person's vision for a place.

Mustafa Ataturk is credited with being the founder of modern Turkey. The American equivalent would be George Washington.

Ataturk's mausoleum sat on what was, at a time prior to skyscrapers, the highest point in Ankara. There are many accounts of his leadership and vision. Relocating the country's capital from Istanbul to Ankara was his strategic decision. My favorite Ataturk story was the account of how his pocket watch saved his life.

In 1915, during the battle at Gallipoli, ANZAC troops landed on

Turkish soil. Their intent was to secure a sea route to Russia.

Positioned in a trench in Gallipoli, Ataturk instructed his soldiers to wait for his signal to attack. He told them to watch for him to stand up in the trench and raise his whip; that would be their signal to take action.

But when Ataturk stood up to give the signal, a sniper's shot hit him in the heart. The bullet went through his uniform, but was blocked from fatally hitting his heart by his pocket watch. The timepiece absorbed the bullet's blow, and was smashed. The placement of his watch saved his life.

"It wasn't his time," Hudson quipped.

Images, photographs, and profile renderings of Ataturk are prevalent throughout Turkey. His image reminded me vaguely of the actor Bela Lugosi. We saw more than a few cars with Ataturk's profile on the back window. In most restaurants there was a framed portrait or black-and-white photograph hanging on the wall. In a rug showroom, the salesman was proud to display a woven rendition of Ataturk in shades of burgundy, gold and cream yarns.

My home office is decorated with inspirational quotes. One stands out as I think of President Ataturk: "A leader takes people where they want to go. A great leader takes people where they don't necessarily want to go, but ought to be."

He was the first president of Turkey and, though he died in 1938, he is much beloved today. His passion, vision, and active leadership transformed Turkey, changing its destiny.

Hierapolis — Pamukkale

There were times, like when we were in Hierapolis and Pamukkale that I wondered, how did I not know about these places? Was I too centered on my own life? Myself? Just the United States?

Gökçe prefaced our walk around the archaeological site with an explanation of the importance of this area in Turkish history.

"Hierapolis means sacred city. It was believed to be founded by the god Apollo. In the midst of the ruins is what is left of the Temple of Apollo," she explained. "Like the Oracle at Delphi in Greece, the Apollo temple was built over a fault, where chemical vapors and gasses escaped. These fumes often caused hallucinations, so we are told, helping to inspire the oracles."

A historic place of healing, it was one of the first modern spa centers of the ancient world. The ruins of Hierapolis, in southwest Turkey, were 25 km (15 miles) from the Aegean Sea.

We started and ended our visit to Hierapolis at Pamukkale. Bright white travertine terraces contained turquoise blue pooled water. Hundreds of tourists kicked off their shoes and waded in. They moved slowly and we heard a few say the moss made the walking slippery. Hudson and I removed our shoes and stepped in. We shuffled along, creating small ripples in the extremely warm thermal water.

There were a lot of tourists at Pamukkale; it was a visually stunning place. Many would approach the edge of the limestone and calcium plateau and strike 1940s-esque glamour poses. The perfectly white stone and teal blue pools were the dramatic backdrop.

There was one lifeguard who stood on land, overseeing the terraces. Blindingly white and shiny slick, the surface could be confused for snow. Many tourists went to the outer edge. There were no fences or indicators, except for the fear of falling off! The lifeguard's shrill whistle was a constant background sound.

Healing with water at the Asclepion in Pergamum was the reason people in the fourth century BC traveled to this city near Bergama. Asclepion was named for a Greek God. This healing temple offered sacred springs in which to bathe. Now the world's most famous ancient medical center, many of the methods used there and then are still in practice today.

While walking through the Asclepion, we saw a small pond where a family of turtles, dragonflies, and frogs gathered. I remembered reading that frogs were a sign of health and balance. Although we stood in ruins, we stood on ancient healing grounds.

From that vantage point, Gökçe pointed to the hilltop and told us that to visualize an altar there.

"Along with the pocket watch that saved Ataturk's life in Gallipoli, the Pergamon altar is in a museum in Berlin," she said with annoyance. "The Germans won't give back what rightfully belongs to Turkey."

She caused me to think about where things belong, and to whom. Who owns artifacts? The people and/or countries who can afford to resurrect them? Do they belong where they are originally found?

A few months prior to our trip, I had read a story about excavators "discovering" the Gates of Hell in Hierapolis. Was it a site of the Oracle of Delphi? Was it named for the fumes it emitted?

In Hierapolis, it was easy to find that spot amidst ruins. A working red crane was the marker for the Gates of Hell. We watched as an Italian excavation crew worked within the fenced area. I thought about my visits to museums in a way I had never thought about before. Though I had not been to the Pergamon Museum in Berlin, listening to Gökçe's passionate opinion about its rightful place caused me to pause. If the country of origin wants their artifacts back, should they be returned?

Another benefit to travel — it raises questions that not only had I never asked, I had never even thought to ask. A similar question was raised when we went to Troy.

Troy

As an English major in college, I can remember reading Homer's The Iliad and The Odyssey. At that time, I thought Troy was a fictional place, and the Trojan War a legend. Thirty years later, I found myself in Troy with my son who had just read The Odyssey the preceding year, as an eighth grader. Troy and the Trojan War are real.

With a two-story high wooden Trojan horse in the background,

Gökçe gathered the group prior to walking into the city.

"For a very long time it was not known if the city of Troy and the stories of the decade-long Trojan War were fact or fiction," she explained.

So I wasn't alone in not knowing if Troy was real or fake.

Troy was different than any other archaeological site we had previously been to. We followed a path that eventually became a raised planked walkway overlooking the ruins.

The guidebook taught us that "few areas of Turkey have been as thoroughly excavated as Troy." The site, just west of Canakkale in northwest Turkey, dated from 4000 BC until 300 AD.

To date, nine Troys have been excavated. At one point during our late-day visit, a strong, dry wind from the west whipped up. Gökçe asked us to face the wind. As we did, she pointed. In front of us were acres and acres of farmland. We could see the Aegean in the distance.

"When Troy was an active city, the Aegean came all the way up here," she said, indicating the nearby hill. "That is five km."

Hudson was excited to be in Troy. He mentioned his history teacher, Mr. Seeley, and his Language Arts teacher, Ms. Cahill, more than once.

"Mom, when we get home I want to send these pictures to them," he said. "Especially that one," he said, pointing to the open area where Roman numerals I —IX indicated the nine excavation layers of Troy.

Gökçe's face turned serious.

"Troy was raped in the 1880s," she stated solemnly.

I was startled by her choice of words.

"See that trench?" she said as she pointed to the clearing just off the planked walkway. "An amateur, Heinrich Schliemann from Germany, showed up and started digging, looking for treasures from Troy number two. He ruined the site. At the time, the Ottoman Empire leaders did not care. He found some gold and silver jewelry and took it back to Germany."

Gökçe's bitterness about artifacts removed from her country was palpable. We understood where she believed the treasures from Troy should be housed.

Something caught my eye as we ambled toward the exit. A single bright red poppy swayed in the wind. Hudson and I stopped and took a picture, remarking how such a delicate flower could survive and thrive in such a place.

Ephesus

"This will be the highlight of your trip to Turkey," Gökçe said, smiling.

Hudson and I exchanged looks.

"Please wear comfortable walking shoes. We will be in Ephesus for more than two hours. Also, prepare yourself for crowds and the heat," she advised.

On the bus, I kicked off my flip flops and slipped on cotton socks and sneakers. Hudson and I liberally applied suntan lotion. We were ready for the best day in Turkey.

A nine a.m. departure from the hotel brought us to Ephesus before the sun was unforgiving. From the guidebook, we learned Ephesus was one of the greatest ruined cities in the western world. At one time, it was a chief port. The Bible lists it as one of the seven cities of the Revelation.

Before we explored the ancient white marble streets, from the 4th century BC, Gökçe gathered the tour group off the bus for a short history lesson. We stood by waiting for the others to get off the bus. Hudson laughed and pointed to a sign across the street.

"I need to get a picture of that," he said as he took out the camera.

Vendors lined the roadway across from the Ephesus entrance. The sign above one table of merchandise read "Genuine Fake Watches."

Gökçe led us through the site. I took mental notes.

"Re-read the Bible, refresh my knowledge of Greek and Roman empires, research Ephesians, and look into taking an online class with Coursera about the ancient world," I said to myself.

"In the first century BC," Gökçe began, "Ephesus was a huge city with more than 250,000 people. One of the ways we know this is by studying that."

Pointing to an open-air theatre, she instructed us to join her there and have a seat.

"Populations of cities could be determined by the size of the theatres," she explained. "This theatre held about 25,000 spectators."

Seated on cool marble in the shade, I looked around, thinking: "This is the oldest place I have ever been to."

Then I glanced at Hudson. Here we were in Ephesus. I had seen pictures in history books, but here we were able to learn firsthand about this magnificent city. I'd known about the importance of education already — but now I knew it very deeply.

"We are sitting in an excavated city, and these are the ruins and evidence of that city," Gökçe said with awe in her voice. "Can anyone tell me if this theatre was open-air or covered?"

All sixteen of us looked up. There was nothing on top of the structure to connect a roof. We took a few stray guesses, and we were all wrong.

"You all looked up when I asked that question," Gökçe said, smiling. "You need to look down, for drainage. That is how you can tell if it was covered or not. Only an outdoor theatre would need drainage, like you see here."

As we all looked down to see the drainage, another tour group stopped and looked at the theatre. A cat jumped up on the wall, presumably to be pet or fed, or both; a mother and daughter swatted at it and Hudson and I exchanged looks. We had packed bread from breakfast to feed whatever stray cats or dogs we came across. The cats in Turkey acted like dogs, approachable and lingering. We gave away a lot of bread in Ephesus.

The highlights of Ephesus were many. We walked the steps of the Library of Celsus, built in 114 AD, and studied the statues in the front niches; Sophia (wisdom), Arete (virtue), Ennoia (intellect), and Episteme (knowledge). We walked up to the Temple of Hadrian and the Gate of Hercules. All these sites reminded me to re-study ancient history.

We walked down the slick marble-paved streets, careful not to stumble on the deep grooves left from chariot wheels. I overheard a man say to his wife, "We are walking in the steps of St. Paul."

Off the main street, Gökçe pulled us aside to show us where the men of Ephesus went to socialize. Behind a marble wall were a line of marble seats with key-hole openings every three or four feet. Under the openings was a dry aqueduct.

"This is why we shake hands with our right hand," Gökçe said. "The left hand was used for wiping."

We were looking at the first public toilet.

Traveling with my son does bring up the question of toilets. When he was very young, he would accompany me into the ladies room. As he got older, this felt awkward, but letting him walk into the men's room unattended filled me with doubt and fear.

"Talk to no one and keep your eyes on your own body or the floor," I would advise him. As of this writing, I have no bathroom horror stories to share, just stories about the facilities themselves.

Hudson's bathroom acumen started in an airplane. Up until that point he had used toilets and urinals at home or school, the occasional restaurant or friends' house. Even outdoors, when necessary.

In France, Hudson learned the difference between a toilet and bidet, and in Hungary we both used our first square toilet. Throughout parts of Europe, Turkey and Morocco, the toilet was nonexistent. Instead, we entered a room the size of a broom closet. In the center, a drainage hole was the target. On either side of the hole in the ground was rough cement or a tiled floor. These bathrooms helped us develop strength in our thigh muscles and our open-mindedness.

While observing the toilets in Ephesus, Hudson and I recalled toilet talk at the United Nations in Manhattan. What we learned there was the importance of sanitation. We take private toilets and access for granted. The statistic shared by U.N. researchers was shocking: One-third of the world, more than two billion people, lack access to sanitation. More shocking and terrible was the fact that diarrheal disease kills more children annually than AIDS, malaria, and measles combined.

Traveling broadens our knowledge, no doubt. More importantly, it broadens our awareness and empathy to world struggles. To learn is not enough. When confronted with statistics like these, I ask what we can do. We tell and retell our stories, what we learned, who we met, and we ask how can we help? It is more than money; it is cultural shifts that need to happen, on both sides. Ours is awareness and then action.

The talk of toilets in Ephesus prompted several potty jokes and introspection about the evolution of ideas and design. We were universal in our agreement about the intelligence behind the invention, and stalled about what we could do about making it universal.

Gökçe continued to educate us on the historical importance of Ephesus.

"Built by ancient Greek colonists in the tenth century BC, Ephesus was a thriving metropolis and identified as one of the seven churches of Asia in the Book of Revelations. It was completely abandoned in the fifteenth century AD," she told us. "The largest collection of Roman ruins in the eastern Mediterranean are here, and only fifteen percent of it has been excavated, predominately by Austrians."

We could tell by the tone of her voice that she was not happy with who was behind the excavations.

Walking through Ephesus, I understood how fleeting life is. Inspirational quotes about carpe diem made sense.

We exited Ephesus late morning. We reboarded the bus bound for Meryemana, home of the Virgin Mary. It was a slow four-mile climb up into thick evergreen woods. The bus hugged the inside of the narrow roadway as serpentine curves offered panoramic views.

The last thing we saw in Ephesus was the keyhole opening for the Ephesian toilets. The first thing we saw in Meryemana was a massive keyhole opening in the ground, an ancient form of collecting water.

A stream ran under the tiny stone house of Mother Mary. The water is believed to be blessed. Hudson and I carried two empty water bottles to collect blessed water from the artisanal well.

The property was charming and bucolic and the home so small we were through it in under a minute, including time for Hudson to hesitate to study a kneeling, praying woman. He wasn't sure if she was real or a prop. She lifted her eyes and met his gaze. She was real.

Butterflies fluttered in and out of the surrounding gardens and woods while cicadas hummed in the trees. The air smelled sweet with fragrant flowers. The property and home were modest and immaculate and there was an air of reverential quietness.

We filled our two bottles with holy water. Standing back, we watched a young mother hoist her daughter up to the font. They both put their mouths under the running water and splashed their faces. An older man, his hands formed into cups, scooped the water onto his feet. Others put their hands in the water and made the sign of the cross on their foreheads or over their hearts.

We held onto our bottles of water and walked along the cobblestone path to the prayer wall. I felt emotion in the air. The wall, twenty feet long by eight feet high, was puffy with white pieces of paper in all sizes. The cumulative prayers gave the appearance of a vertical arts and crafts project, homespun and ragged. Prayers written in countless languages, some legible, were tied to each other with tissue or paper.

Feeling weepy, I pulled out two pieces of paper from my bag and handed one to Hudson. We sat on a nearby rock wall, paused, and wrote out our prayers.

In blue ink I printed in all capital letters, HELP ME SEE. A tear rolled down my cheek and plopped onto the page like a punctuation mark.

Without speaking, we folded and rolled them. They looked like tiny cigars. We approached the wall and attached our intentions. Using the plastic wrapper from our water bottles, we tied our prayers to the thousands of others.

I took a picture of Hudson in his grass-green t-shirt attaching his prayer to the wall. The profile of his face is sweet and tender.

Gökçe greeted us as we walked up to the bus.

"Get ready for the best lunch in an unexpected place," she said, smiling mischievously. She offered no other information.

We took our seats on the bus, quiet and reflective.

With Ephesus, Meryemana, and the Aegean Sea behind us, the bus headed inland, to the Kozak region. Feeling weary after a morning experiencing great history, Hudson and I gazed quietly out the window at the heavily forested and mountainous landscape. It felt like we were going on a camping trip!

We arrived in the tiny town of Gobeller, curious about the unknown plans for lunch. Exiting the bus, we huddled under the shade of an enormous tree in the center of town. The mayor appeared, and we were enthusiastically greeted. He shook everyone's hand and smiled.

He spoke no English, and with the exception of hello and thank you, we spoke no Turkish. We smiled at each other.

Gökçe divided us into smaller groups, and told us we would be taken to the homes of local townspeople. "Lunch is all homemade, all vegetarian, and our treat!" she announced happily.

Hudson and I were partnered with two married Australian couples, Alan and Jan and Michael and Jennifer. We were guided up a one-way residential street. Around a bend in the road, an older woman wearing a white apron smiled as we approached. Standing behind a table, she waved her hand, presenting the textiles and t-shirts she was selling.

We stopped and looked at her colorful offerings, but did not buy anything. We kept walking and turned left into a small courtyard. Two cats, sleeping like yin and yang, woke up sleepily and let us pass without care.

The courtyard was immaculate and bright, the perimeter was decorated with flower pots. We walked up a single flight of white steps onto a wooden deck. Directed with hand signals, we sat at a table outdoors, under a roof overhang. Set with white plates, drinking glasses, and utensils, the table was covered with a crisp white cotton tablecloth. It felt casual and comfortable. We were each instructed to sit in one of the six chairs.

Gökçe introduced Aysen, the mother and cook, who had shyly peeked her ruddy face out of the door way. Her head was covered in a scarf. She smiled as she handed us bottles of water.

Although it was a sunny, hot day, the porch was cool. It was simply decorated with potted plants, red and pink geraniums, all in full bloom. One pot had the Turkish flag on a stick propped into the soil. The red ground cloth of the flag played off the flower color. In the near distance, two or three houses away, four storks in a nest studied us.

Aysen reappeared at the doorway. The six of us looked over at her, Pavlovian, anticipating. She handed us each a bowl of tarhana. Gökçe told us tarhana was a traditional Turkish soup made with yogurt, onions, tomatoes and green peppers. A bowl of cut white bread was quietly placed in the center of the table.

"Your lunch will be free and all vegetarian," Gökçe reminded us from the doorway. "Enjoy! I am off to check on the other groups."

And with that, she left us.

The hosting family did not speak English. We smiled and nodded our thanks and appreciation. The soup was light and tasty. As we sipped, a plate of sigara boregi, cheese rolls, was placed on the table. I put my soup spoon down and reached for the cigar-shaped pastry. The toasted crust flaked off in my mouth, and the moist cheese and parsley stuffing was warm. Delicious!

We heard talking coming from inside the house. Aysen's two daughters came to the doorway carrying plates of cigirtma (eggplant) and bulgur pilavi (rice pilaf).

We later learned Sing was thirteen years old and Sammy, her

older sister, eighteen.

The midday call to prayer sounded from a nearby mosque as a butterfly landed on one of the red geraniums. Two of the four storks in the nearby nest stood, stretching their long, skinny white legs.

Storks. It was funny to think about storks, having grown up with images of them as cartoon characgters. Flying messengers carrying sacks of mail, or a baby, snuggly packed in a white bundle. In Turkey, storks were messengers as well. We were told when you see a stork, it was a sign that more travel would be in your future.

A rooster crowed, and Michael shared an anecdote he heard in Nepal.

"If a rooster crows at any other time than daybreak," he started, "then they are meant for the pot, as they don't know what they are there for."

I felt like I could feel Turkey. The authenticity and warmth of this family was palpable. Using hand gestures, thumbs up and kissed fingertips, we smiled at them appreciatively. We kept eating, which was the highest compliment.

Aysen appeared at the doorway with yet another plate. Sarma — rolled vine leaves stuffed with rice, onion and parsley were stacked neatly on the square white plate. I took one and ate it. The firm vine leaves snapped when I bit into the dense interior. Three bites and I took another. This was my favorite food.

Individual plates of sarayli, a walnut and honey Baklava-type dessert was served, but I was still in sarma heaven. Hudson ate his sarayli, I think, without breathing. I offered him mine in exchange for more sarma, a successful and satisfying swap for both of us.

Through hand gestures, we were offered and accepted cups of Turkish tea. The hot, caramel-colored tea arrived in a classic Turkish tulip glass on a small formal saucer.

After tea, we were invited into the house. Aysen pointed to our feet. We understood, and took our shoes off before entering.

The spartan and humble home was modest and immaculate. I pointed to a framed embroidered flower on the wall. Aysen smiled and proudly patted her chest, indicating she had made it.

The ceiling was higher than ours at home. It was paneled with a shiny, light tan wood. Two sofas sat against the walls on a tan carpet. I looked down the hall. Aysen nodded, and picked up a two-liter-plastic Pepsi bottle. Without words, she showed me how she refilled it with water and plastic flowers. Using recycled materials, she had created a door stopper.

I was guided across the hall to the bedroom Sing and Sammy shared. An acoustic guitar hung on the pale pink wall.

Sammy, standing with me in the doorway, smiled. She pointed to the guitar and herself. It was her guitar.

Sedef, the father, stood back and quietly observed. His wife and two daughters took us through the rest of their home silently. It was an intimate afternoon with sweet and kind people.

"Tesekkur ederim," we said, with varying degrees of aptitude, and walked back to the bus.

Back at the tree in the center of town, we gathered waiting for our other travelers to return from their lunches.

While we waited, I felt another pang of motherhood when one of the people on the tour asked Hudson a question.

"What do you want to be when you grow up?"

I stood by, benignly listening. He's growing up and doesn't need me to speak for him, I thought. Words from a New York Times op-ed came to mind about parenting: "…you are doing it best when you are teaching them to leave you." I could feel the bittersweet truth in those words.

Hudson replied, "I want to work for Doctors without Borders someday."

I felt bittersweet pride. This is what I wanted after all, right? To raise a citizen of the world?

Gallipoli

Three years ago, we visited the Normandy Beaches. I didn't believe another battlefield and cemetery could affect me as deeply as that one in northern France did. I underestimated Gallipoli, the site of one of the bloodiest battles of World War I, where more than 500,000 allied (Australian, British, French, Indian, and New Zealander) and Turkish soldiers had fought and died.

We crossed to the Gallipoli peninsula after spending ten days in Asian Turkey. The ferry carried people and vehicles. The water was characteristically rough and choppy as we crossed back to European Turkey and onto to the Gallipoli peninsula. The distance from Canakkale to the peninsula was short (1200 meters or 3,937 feet across). The white-capped waters of the Dardanelles demanded that we hold onto the handrail the entire time. The narrow and windy strait was at one time called Hellespont for its rough current.

Small and powerful, the Dardanelles was a strategic location in 1915 as it provided a sea route to Russia. I needed to study a map to see the connections. The Dardanelles provided entry to the Sea of Marmara, and from there the Bosporus strait connected to the Black Sea.

We docked on the Gallipoli peninsula. Gökçe told us the ANZACS who landed there in 1915 had trained on remarkably different terrain. They had arrived in Cairo and trained in the desert. The hilly terrain of the peninsula was one of their many setbacks.

Hudson and I walked off the bus. A single pine tree stood in the midst of a cemetery. The Lone Pine Cemetery was crowded with visitors quietly reflecting and reading gravestones.

As we slowly walked along the manicured plots, we paused to read the inscriptions on the tombstones. As in Normandy, the ages of the soldiers struck me — they had been teenaged boys. There I stood on the graves of young men who had probably just started shaving when they died. I looked over at Hudson, my eyes watering. I felt a lump in my throat. Wiping away tears, I felt a pang of grief for the mothers who had lost their sons there. I found myself shaking my head no — this was not fair.

Nearby, two women from our group, Vera from Mumbai and Olga from the U.S. but originally from Ecuador, were talking. I overheard Vera say, "I believe if there was no religion, there would be no war."

Like Normandy, there were no distractions from feeling this place.

When we arrived at ANZAC cove, the bus was solemnly quiet. I heard some sniffling and someone blew their nose. Gökçe told us the two sides, the "Johnnies" from Australia and New Zealand and the "Mehmets" of Turkey, had a mutual respect for each other and still do to this day.

As an American, I was moved by this place. I could not trace any connection from my immediate family there. Many of our fellow travelers, Australians, were naming uncles and grandparents who had fought and died there.

Quietly and slowly we had stopped in front of tombstones, reading the inscriptions. "Duty Bravely Done" and "Death Cannot Long Divide," "He Careth for Them" and "Dear is the spot to me where my beloved son rests, my ANZAC hero. Mother."

All but three tombstones faced the sparkling water of the Aegean Sea. Three Muslim Indian soldiers were buried at a 90-degree angle to their comrades, facing southeast to Mecca. Gökçe told us that Muslims are buried on their sides with their faces looking toward Mecca in Saudi Arabia.

Hudson and I did not speak. With the Aegean and the cemetery behind us, we walked toward a granite memorial inscribed with emotional words from Ataturk:

"THOSE HEROES THAT SHED THEIR BLOOD
AND LOST THEIR LIVES...
   YOU ARE NOW LYING IN THE SOIL OF A FRIENDLY COUNTRY.

THEREFORE REST IN PEACE.

THERE IS NO DIFFERENCE BETWEEN THE JOHNNIES

AND THE MEHMETS TO US WHERE THEY LIE SIDE BY SIDE

HERE IN THIS COUNTRY OF OURS…

YOU, THE MOTHERS

WHO SENT THEIR SONS FROM FAR AWAY COUNTRIES

WIPE AWAY YOUR TEARS;

YOUR SONS ARE NOW LYING IN OUR BOSOM AND ARE IN PEACE.

AFTER HAVING LOST THEIR LIVES ON THIS LAND THEY HAVE

BECOME OUR SONS AS WELL."

-ATATURK 1934

More emotion was ahead as we boarded the bus.

Our final stop in Gallipoli was in the middle of the peninsula, on the battlefields. We walked past reconstructed trenches and up to a statue of Ataturk, raised whip in hand. The story of the pocket watch that saved his life was etched at the base of the monument.

As we stood on the well-wooded and dusty battlefield, we were distracted. A swarm of people, young Turkish army men and women touring the site, surrounded us, their young faces ardent. I felt powerful emotions as I looked at them. I saw only a few years' difference between my son and those soldiers.

"Mom," Hudson said.

I looked at him, filled with feelings of tenderness and fierce protection.

"Yes?"

"It is new souls on top of old souls," he said.

I nodded.

"This is more powerful than Normandy," he continued. "Soldiers died on both sides only because their governments told them to fight. There was no real reason. They were pawns for greedy empires."

Sometimes my feelings are so deep and powerful that it is hard to stay present with them. At that moment I identified with the pain those mothers felt at the loss of their sons, their babies. If "service is love made visible," at this battlefield, who or what was served?

It was our last day with the tour group. The bus journey back to Istanbul was protracted, due to traffic. Hudson and I played cards. I lost more games of Rummy on this stretch than ever before. Some of our fellow passengers made comments.

"Laura, is Hudson beating you again?" Jan asked from a few rows back.

"Yes, the humiliation continues," I laughed, nodding.

Hudson laid down a six card straight, and Steve, a friendly Australian seated behind us said, "I saw that coming and it warmed my heart. Well played, Hudson."

As the bus idled in stopped traffic, Gökçe stood up at the front and offered more insights on Turkish life, geography, Muslim culture and the current protest movement in Istanbul.

"As we talked about earlier, there are some people in Turkey who are not happy with the current prime minister. He has been in power for ten years and our elections are every four years. We will see what happens then," she said. "In Turkey, voting is mandatory, regardless of what your profession is. I live on a bus and I do not have an excuse. If I know I am going to be traveling when there are elections, I have to send in my vote ahead of time. If I don't, I am fined."

Alan and Jan from Australia offered, in unison, "It is the same in Australia, voting is compulsory."

Hudson did some research. Mandatory voting is law in more than twenty-five countries worldwide. That's another reason I liked traveling with a tour group, I learned new facts and gained fresh perspectives. Hudson and I talked about low voter turnout in the U.S. Perhaps our country would consider mandotory voting?

Along the way, I had asked a few of our fellow tour travelers which they preferred, taking tours or independent travel?

Alan's answer was: "I like taking a tour and then having a few days of independent travel. I have done both and like the combination."

This was our first organized tour; my unsupported impressions were dispelled, replaced with a positive opinion.

Upon our return to Istanbul, we hugged and said emotional goodbyes to our fellow travelers. We swapped email and phone numbers with a few. We were off for four days of independent exploration.

Istanbul, Part Two

Julie and Graham, our friends from London, joined us in Istanbul. It was their first time to Turkey. Julie researched and found a cozy boutique hotel. It was in the heart of the Sultanahmet neighborhood, or the old town, as it is referred to by locals. With one place to stay and an open schedule, Hudson and I could visit with Julie and Graham and revisit Istanbul.

We stayed at the Hotel Empress Zoe, a tiny boutique hotel with a fifteenth century hammam on the property. A stone wall in the lobby was shared with the hammam.

Our small room had rustic wood floors. Turkish rugs hung on the wall as art. There were two marble bathrooms, one with a modern sink and shower, and the second with an ancient cistern.

The garden was the highlight of the hotel. Every morning, a buffet style breakfast was presented in the miniscule but modern kitchen. We would carry our plates and drinks outdoors, walk out on the gravel and slate path and be transformed. The open-air garden was cocooned with vegetation. The rounded rooftop of the hammam peeked up. Several cats sat patiently nearby ready for crumbs. We heard the sound of trickling water. Nestled under vines and small trees were two cisterns. Small marble-top tables with chairs were dotted throughout the shaded garden. Until one of the five calls to prayer sounded, I had forgotten we were in the heart of a city with eleven million other people.

Our first night with Julie and Graham, we ate dinner near the hotel at an outdoor café. The waiter arrived with a pillow and placed it on the table.

"Bread for you," he said, and walked away to get menus.

The pillow bread looked like a misshaped football, a light tan and uneven bumpy surface. The four of us studied the bread when we heard a voice from behind us.

"Is this your first time to Istanbul?" A young man leaning over the railing asked us.

He indicated the carpet store next to the restaurant, adding, "I work right here."

"Where are you from?" he asked us.

"The U.S. and the U.K.," we answered together.

He told us he was Turkish, but not from Istanbul.

"I am from Van, in the eastern part of Turkey. I am Kurdish," he shared. "I am happy to see tourists here. Our business has dropped thirty percent since the protests started in May."

With the start of Ramadan two days away, Julie asked him, "Will you be fasting during Ramadan?"

"I will try. It is very hard with the heat not to take a drink, but I will do my best," he said.

I studied his face, warm and brown, highlighted by dark brown-black eyes with eyelashes so thick and black they looked like he was wearing mascara.

"Your carpets look beautiful," Julie said indicating the window display of woven red, gold and brown rugs. "Do you like selling rugs?"

"It is hard to know what people want," he said, leaving us to help a customer.

Once done marveling at the bread, Julie tore a piece off the end. A poof of hot air was released, revealing a hollow interior. It had the texture and taste of pita bread. We ate the entire loaf and asked for a second.

Over dinner, we talked about what we wanted to see and do for the next few days. Touching Asian Istanbul was a goal for Julie and Graham. We decided that would be the first activity. The following morning, we walked toward the Hippodrome, where all the tourist activities were. We looked for tourist-friendly helpers. They were easy to spot in their light blue tee shirts with ASK ME in bold black letters on the front.

They told us how to buy tokens for the tram and instructed us on how to get to the dock to catch a ferry.

Graham suggested taking the worker's ferry to Asia, to save money while getting a feeling for authentic Turkish life. We walked up to the machine selling tokens for the ferry, and immediately a Turkish man came up and helped us with the transaction. His timing was perfect. We bought tokens and ran for the ferry. I was the last one on board.

We crossed the Bosporus with only a few other passengers. The slow-moving ferry carved through the water and headed east. It shared the narrow passageway with enormous tankers.

Arrival onto the Asian side of Istanbul was uneventful. There were no signs of being in a different continent. I had imagined a brightly colored billboard: Welcome to Asia, largest and most populous continent on Earth! We stayed for about an hour, long enough for Julie and Graham to say they touched Asia. Walking back to the dock to board the ferry to go back to European Istanbul, Graham suggested trying out a new restaurant he had heard about.

Back in Europe — no welcome sign on that side either — we

asked a few people how to get to the Lokanta Maya restaurant. We wound our way through the streets of the Karakoy neighborhood, which sits on the Bosporus. Thirty minutes of walking and we were there.

Once inside, we admired the mosaic tile work on the walls and floor and ordered lunch. Graham and Hudson had the Scorpio soup, a white spicy broth with chunks of fish, and Julie and I had eggplant. I ate some form of eggplant every day in Turkey, and never got tired of it.

Lunch was tasty. It was refreshing to get away from the touristy areas. But the most magical meal was yet to come.

For dinner that night, the four of us sat outside, on the rooftop of a seafood restaurant in Sultanahmet. It was dusk and the sunset was a soft pinky orange. It was July 8, the first night of Ramadan, one of the five pillars of Islam. For observant Muslims, it was the start of a month-long fast.

Hagia Sophia sang the evening call to prayer. The Blue Mosque answered back. The two mosques were in harmony. One sang and finished, and the other chanted and finished. It was a lyrical wave ebbing and flowing. They were talking to each other!

We learned later that the two mosques were always live, never recorded. The call to prayer message was always the same: "It is a small thing to give yourself to God. Come to prayer."

When the call to prayer ended, netting between the two minarets on the Blue Mosque illuminated the words: "Merhaba Ya Sehri Ramazan!" or Welcome Ramadan!

We sat quietly and listened. We could feel the call to prayer humming in the air.

Suddenly, the Turkish man seated behind us, who had translated the lit-up mosque message for us moments before, said, "Look, over there! Venus is out!"

Getting a hammam — a Turkish bath — while in Turkey was another trip goal. I had loved the hammam experience in Morocco and wanted to compare it to one in Turkey.

The entrances were separate for men and women, as they were in Morocco. The experiences were similar. Both were sensual, relaxing and soothing. I sat naked on the marble bench as the attendant splashed me with cool water, washing away the day's dirt and sweat. The feeling of self-consciousness about my nudity was washed away, too. I looked around and saw naked women and girls of all shapes and sizes around me.

It sounds like it could be sexy. It wasn't. It was robust and cleansing, and methodically deliberate. The lighting was low and soft, and the smell of water sat in the humid air. White marble sinks, benches, and large, low slabs for massages were offset by gold hardware. Arched doorways connected the washing room I was in to a lounge area. Women wrapped in white robes and white cotton towel turbans sat back and drank water with floating lemon slices.

With every splash of water, the woman who attended me also got wet. She wore a white cotton toga that clung to her shiny brown skin. Kind and nurturing, she confidently moved my arm upright as she rigorously scrubbed it. On her right hand, she wore an exfoliating mitt. She rubbed my upper arm rough and fast. Small bits of dead skin fell to the ground. I was mortified. I had taken a shower that morning. Was I that dirty from walking around Istanbul?

She spoke no English. My eyes squinted, my head tilted, and my mouth exhibited an embarrassed expression. I looked into her eyes as if to say, "Sorry I am so dirty." I pointed to the growing mound of dead skin on the clean white marble floor.

Her response surprised me. Smiling, she shook her head excitedly, "Goot, goot, goot," she said.

I learned about perspective that day.

CHAPTER 11

Food

I'm a lover of questions. Perhaps one of my favorites is, "what are we going to eat?"

Hudson and I love adventure, which includes trying new and different foods. We look forward to new spices and food combinations, and we appreciate the presentation.

In Morocco we were continually delighted. We drank Moroccan whiskey, ate bread embedded with rocks, scooped stew from a tagine, and silently devoured cumin-covered kefta. Many nights while we ate dinner, our table was sprinkled with red rose petals, while the fifth and final call to prayer summoned believers in the background. Morocco was one of the most poetic places I have ever been.

Our first adventure in Moroccan dining was an antidote to Hudson's upset stomach. It wouldn't be until we returned to the United States, two weeks later, that we knew the reason for his nausea. His pediatrician diagnosed Hudson with salmonella. The possible source was two hot dogs he ate in terminal 1 at JFK airport prior to flying to Casablanca.

The van had pulled over several times on the ride from Casablanca airport to Rabat when Hudson indicated the need to vomit. The dinner at the Rabat riad was toned down to help settle his nausea.

Even toned-down Moroccan food was still exciting despite his queasy stomach. We both ate squab for the first time. Squab, or pigeon, is lean dark meat, easily digestible, and very tasty and juicy. Served on the side was our first taste of Moroccan couscous, a semolina pasta-rice combination that feels like you are eating millions of tiny bits of rice in one forkfull. Though the intent was to serve something less spicy for Hudson, the meal was sumptuous and flavorful and helped settle his stomach.

Tagine cooking in Morocco was as ubiquitous as pizza is in America. And just as we never get tired or bored with eating pizza at home, we never tired of the tagine cooking.

In a striking comparison to roadside dining at home, Chakir brought us to a gas station rest stop. "This is where we will have lunch," he said. "The tagine cooking and bread are excellent here."

He was right.

Picnic tables were shaded by an extended roof. It looked like a large outdoor gazebo. Several yards away, cars and trucks sped by on the highway. At our feet, well-fed cats sauntered expectantly.

We walked up to a counter and were greeted warmly by a man who was ready to take our order. Behind him, in the open kitchen, a woman wearing a white apron and casually tied scarf deftly maneuvered a large long wooden spatula, like the ones used in American pizza kitchens.

Hudson, Chakir and I stood and watched as she shoveled bumpy round pita-like bread from the small arched opening of the fire oven. She brought the bread to the counter quickly jerking her hand to slide it off, just like a pizza at home.

Her next steps were like nothing we had ever seen before. Her gloved hands picked up the freshly baked flat bread and slammed it against the tiled counter top. Hudson and I looked at each other and then at Chakir.

"She is removing the rocks," he said smiling.

"Rocks?" Hudson and I said in unison.

"Yes. Rocks. She presses them into the dough before she bakes it.

The rocks hold the heat and help to bake the bread evenly throughout," he explained.

The bread was placed before the three of us. There were no rocks, only cratered indentations.

"Hudson, carry the plate and follow me," Chakir instructed.

Walking to the next open counter, Chakir suggested tagine for lunch.

Hudson and I were still studying the rock bread. We quietly nodded yes to Chakir. He ordered two tagines for lunch and the three of us made our way to a picnic table.

Chakir tore a piece of the bread off. Hudson and I watched and followed his lead.

"It's great," I said. "That was incredible watching her bang the rocks out of it."

An older man delivered our tagines to the table. He removed the covers, releasing a poof of steam and a luscious aroma. Tagines offer both style and substance.

A functional vessel for slow-cooking meat and vegetables, tagines have two parts. The flat-lipped bottom dish is the base for the conical, round hat sitting on top. The tagine stew we ate was a mix of eggplant and lamb. We dipped the rock bread into the sauce.

The tagine served to us was a matte terra cotta piece. Throughout Morocco, we saw tagines in varying sizes and decoration and many were ornately painted and glazed. They are beautiful empty, too.

Moroccan whiskey was equally ubiquitous as tagine cooking. We smiled every time Hudson said the word "whiskey." The combination of green tea and fresh mint was so refreshing. When we weren't drinking Moroccan whiskey, we drank Cokes or water.

Driving east from the capital city of Rabat, we toured and hiked through Volubilis, a third-century BC, partially excavated Roman city. Our deeply tanned tour guide stood in the shade of one of the few trees at the site and walked and talked with us for more than an hour in the hundred-degree heat. We were tired, hot, and hungry after that excursion. The five-kilometer (three mile) ride to lunch in

Moulay Idriss gave Chakir enough time to tell us about kefta.

"I will take you to a great place for kefta," he said as we sat back in the van, thankful for the air conditioning.

"Sounds good, Chakir. What's kefta?" I asked.

"Oh wait and see, you will love it," he said, smiling into the rearview mirror.

Looking out the van window, we saw soft rolling rural hills. On a hilltop, in the distance, a cluster of white buildings surprised the otherwise tan landscape. The largest building had a grass-green roof.

"That is Moulay Idriss," Chakir said, pointing straight ahead. "It is a pilgrimage site. The building you see with the green roof is the tomb of Moulay Idriss el Akhbal. He was a descendant of the prophet Muhammad."

The approach to the city of Moulay Idriss was stunning. The road created a wide swath arriving in the city, but off to the side and high above it. Chakir pulled over. We got out and enjoyed the bird's eye view of the compressed city.

"Ok?" he asked looking at Hudson and me. "Ready to go and have the best kefta in Morocco?"

Once inside the city, the roads were narrow. Passing outdoor cafés, we saw a young boy seated on the back of a goat. He tapped its rump with a thick piece of hay.

Chakir parked the van. The three of us strolled through the narrow streets and up to a man standing behind a cloud of smoke.

Speaking to us, but loud enough for the man to hear, Chakir said, "This man makes the best kefta in Morocco."

We smiled, and so did the man who stood in front of the smoking barbeque.

"We will all have kefta," Chakir told the man. He promptly placed several sausage-shaped kefta on the grill, causing a big poof of smoke to billow.

Chakir indicated a nearby table. We sat and leaned our elbows on the red and white plastic table-cloth. The centerpiece of the table was a six inch tall canister of cumin. We swatted a few flies away and looked around, taking in the street. Across from our outdoor table was a small shop selling scarves and tourist trinkets. On our left was a mound of shiny oiled olives. Thousands of them.

"Do you like olives?" Chakir asked us.

"Yes, love them," we answered.

Chakir asked the man to bring Cokes and olives to the table.

Along with the drinks and olives, he brought a plate of pita bread. A few moments later, the plate of kefta was served.

We watched and then mimicked Chakir.

He laid a piece of pita on his palm. Using a fork, he stabbed a piece of the five-inch-long piece of freshly cooked kefta onto the pita. He shook some of the table cumin onto the kefta and bit in. Hudson and I did the same. The smell of the nearby BBQ was intense and enticing. We knew it was going to be a treat.

"Wow," Hudson said after his first bite. "This is great, what is it?"

Between bites, Chakir gave us the recipe for kefta: ground beef seasoned with salt and paprika, cumin, parsley and cilantro.

"It is better when it is prepared on an open grill, like here," he explained. "It is easy to make. You could make it when you return home, Laura."

He looked at Hudson and asked, "Is your mom a good cook?"

Hudson hesitated, looked at Chakir and said, "Her cooking skills are rudimentary."

He was right. And when we returned to the U.S., it was one of the first things I cooked, and it was not the same. I made it on the stove top using all the same ingredients.

Hudson's comment aside, the smoky BBQ combined with the heat and quirky charm of Moulay Idriss, while seated next to a mountain of olives with my son and our earthy tour guide, also enhanced the flavor and enjoyment of the kefta.

In Prague, sans tour guide, we had lunch in an outdoor café. Tables were packed tightly together. Nearby, several men smoked cigarettes and spoke in Italian.

Studying the menu, Hudson decided on a margherita flatbread pizza. When the waiter arrived, Hudson ordered the pizza and a Coke. I asked about the goulash.

"The goulash is delicious and I highly recommend it," the young waiter started. "It is served in a brown bread bowl."

"Sounds great," I said. "Can you recommend a Czech beer?"

"Go with the Pilsner Urquell," he suggested. "It is a good solid beer and very popular here."

"Sounds good, goulash and a pilsner for me," I said.

The waiter returned, with a coke and my first Czech beer. The beer was tasty, it had a stronger taste than I was used to, and it was served very cold.

Hudson's pizza came out first. It was served on a flat silver pan that doubled as a plate. Using his fork and knife, he cleanly cut out a slice and took a bite. He smiled his approval.

My lunch was served on a small white plate. The round chunky brown bread was hollowed out, and filled to the brim with soupy goulash. The waiter handed me a large soup spoon.

"That looks good, mom."

"We can share if you want," I suggested.

"Try it first," Hudson said.

Before dipping the spoon into the bread bowl, I touched the sides of the dark bread. It was solid and firm with a little give and created a small wave in the goulash.

I dipped the spoon into the thick stew, gently blew on it before putting it in my mouth.

It was a full-bodied, hearty stew that was robust and flavorful. My American palate craves salty foods. There was little or no salt in the goulash, and I did not miss it. I sipped on another spoonful, and then Hudson wanted to switch dishes.

The goulash was now officially Hudson's. He used a spoon for two mouthfuls and then placed it on the table. He leaned in. He bit into the side of the brown bread bowl. He continued to eat the bowl, squirrel-like, as I got the camera and took pictures of him eating Prague goulash.

Watching Hudson eat, I considered our lifestyle back home. We have an assumption about convenience in America. Convenient and efficient seem to go together; we have come to expect both. When we travel, we relax our expectations. Except for breakfast.

We try to plan for a convenient breakfast as part of our itinerary. Regardless of the size of the hotel, "breakfast included" is one of our preferred requirements. Usually, it is a great value and a necessary start to the day, especially the coffee.

In many of the hotels, there was a hot and cold buffet. Some of the foods offered we recognized — eggs, waffles, bacon, Danish and fruit. Other foods we recognize — just not as breakfast foods.

Both Germany and Austria expanded our understanding of breakfast selections. The spread of hot and cold buffet items included classic breakfast cereals, breads and bagels, eggs, fruits and jams, all standard fare. It was the meat table (not its official name, but could be) that drew our interest and surprise.

Bacon and sausage were presented next to a varied grouping of cold cuts. Hams, salamis, liverwursts, bolognas, and mixed cheeses were neatly arranged on a platter. Though we remarked and marveled at the selection, typically we left the meat table untouched.

My American-ness was often revealed, either in the volume of my speaking, my attire or my accent, but most glaringly at breakfast.

I love coffee. At home, I drink two or three cups every morning. My favorite coffee cup is one that Hudson made and painted. It stands six inches high and looks like a Monet painting on the outside. It's not a cup. It is a mug. On the inside, at the bottom, is a greeting.

Hi.

In Europe, as we sat at the table awaiting buffet instructions, the waiter or waitress simultaneously brought a carafe of coffee to the table. I nodded my head yes to accept the coffee. Looking down at the table setting, I realized not only was there no mug, there was not even a cup. There was a thimble. I realized I would need to fill and refill the tiny coffee cup many times. At that moment I felt very American. I wanted a large mug.

Hudson ate escargot in Paris. There was no coaxing or convincing on my part. We were in a noisy, crowded, and lively bistro in the Opera neighborhood of Paris. The waiter approached the table and asked for our order.

"Escargots, s'il vous plaît," Hudson said with confidence. The waiter nodded and walked away.

"Escargots?" I said looking at Hudson, impressed.

"I'm in France and want to try them. I know they are snails," he said.

"Great. If you don't like them, I can help," I offered.

As we waited for the escargots to arrive, we sat quietly and took in the atmosphere of the bistro. Lively, loud and intimate, it was alive with sounds of clanking silverware and boisterous conversations. The waiter reappeared with twelve escargots on a thin silver tray. Each snail had its own gully, nestled in liquid garlic butter. Placing the plate in front of Hudson, the waiter handed him a silver tool that looked like an eyelash curler.

Hudson took the eyelash curler, aka escargot tool, and grasped his first escargot. Using the tiny two-pronged fork he extracted the snail from the interior of the shell. He re-dipped the snail into the well of garlic butter. Lifting the tiny fork to his mouth, he ate the snail.

"And?" I sat looking at him.

"It's good, Mom. Here, try one."

Hudson adeptly maneuvered another snail from its shell. He handed me the tiny fork with an escargot dripping in butter. I ate it, and nodded at Hudson.

The waiter returned to check on us. We both nodded our mouths full, our delight apparent.

Chapter 12

Coming Home

In the summer of 2014, we stayed home. That is, we didn't leave the United States. Traveling with seventy-three others from Connecticut, Hudson and I went on our first mission trip. Hudson was invited to attend and I was later asked to chaperone.

While all our journeys have been educational, the mission trip brought the learning home. We traveled to eastern Kentucky and learned about the people and geography of Appalachia. We also developed home-building skills.

The trip was about work. The materials for the jobs were funded by grant money, based on need. I had read that mission trips transform people — both the doers and the receivers. I was open to being transformed.

As with earlier travels, we did some research about our destination. A lot has been written and recorded about eastern Kentucky. The focus seemed to be on what was lacking there. There are 3,135 counties in the United States. The 10 poorest are in eastern Kentucky.

Traveling by bus, we left Branford, Connecticut for Neon, Kentucky. By the time we arrived, we had passed through eight states and covered 750 miles. We left the density of I-95 and headed west into New York State, crossing the Newburgh Beacon Bridge.

The inland bus route cut through miles of dense forests with increasing hilly terrain.

This was a trip of firsts for us. It was our first mission trip, a trip designed to be about service. We knew very few people who were going with us. Attending team-building meetings in the months prior to the trip was a requirement. We all knew a little bit about each other. During those meetings, Theresa, the Reverend from the First Congregational Church, coached us. Her goals: Getting us out of our comfort zones, and having no expectations.

Hudson and I had no carpentry skills and would be assigned to work sites where we could find ourselves painting, caulking, nailing, hanging sheetrock, or roofing. All those skills would be learned on-site.

For me, chaperoning meant responsibility. There would be more than fifty youth to serve. Theresa made the directive of the chaperones clear: "This is about the kids, helping them learn skills, but most importantly, how to serve." I felt the weight of this duty and knew I would grow from the experience.

Getting uncomfortable is a life theme for me. Keeping an open mind, meeting new people, and trying different experiences is a lifelong desire. When I asked myself why I wanted to go on this trip, those were my answers.

We traveled in two coach buses. Looking out the window, I saw the sign indicating we were crossing the Mason-Dixon Line. Traveling south on route 81, we left Pennsylvania and entered Maryland. As I was recalling the meaning of that boundary, our bus lost power and the driver told us he was pulling off the exit.

Hudson was on the other bus and the driver radioed and told them we were going to stop and see what the problem was. We were in Hagerstown, Maryland. In the past, I would have been annoyed or impatient with the situation. I wasn't annoyed, and neither were the others. The driver pulled over into a commuter parking lot. We all exited the bus, and stood nearby in the shade awaiting an update.

We were fortunate to have Charlie with us. A mechanic for Ford, he diagnosed and solved the problem in under an hour. From that point on, we all asked, "what can't Charlie do?" By the time we crossed into Clarke County, West Virginia, Charlie was a legend. We had embellished and fictionally expanded his abilities to epic proportions. Charlie was curing cancer and solving world peace.

We stopped for dinner at a Cracker Barrel, and then drove straight through. We pulled into Neon, Kentucky seventeen hours after leaving Connecticut. The rural town was completely dark at 11 p.m. It was understandable how the bus driver took a wrong left turn onto a tight, narrow residential street. Tired and cranky, we watched out the windows as the driver backed the bus across a small grassy area. It was no small feat in the dark, as a creek trickled by, leaving no room for error.

We pulled into Homes, Inc. The headquarters was a white warehouse and garage. In the darkness, we pulled suitcases out of the belly of the bus. Sleepily, the whole group of us wheeled our bags inside. The warehouse was our sleeping accommodations for the week. It smelled like an unaired basement, moldy and mildewed. Four large rooms, outfitted with bunk beds and air conditioning, became our temporary home.

Home took on a new twist for me. Hudson and I stayed home, in the U.S., worked with Homes, Inc., and worked on private homes. On July 4th we attended an independence concert in Whitesburg, Kentucky, featuring the music of Sundy Best. The theme of the concert was "I wanna go home."

I began to wonder, what is home? It is a warm word, or a word that feels soft and loving. I thought a lot about this word and its meaning as we made Neon, population 850, our temporary home.

Statistically, eastern Kentucky is bleak. The New York Times had listed it as the hardest place to live in the country in recent years. The Environmental Protection Agency's carbon-reduction efforts have hit this coal-mining region hard. Coal-related jobs account for only one percent of the population, while it's estimated that at one time, forty percent of the population was employed by coal. Rural

Appalachian Kentucky offers little choice for its citizens. How do people support themselves? And why do they stay?

The poverty of the region has been well documented and it was visible. Downtown Neon, with its empty storefronts, made you think of a time when there was more life in the community. The mass media has covered the poverty in the area for decades and has focused on what was wrong. I was interested to learn what kept people there, what it still had to offer.

Billboards, road signs, and license plates reminded passersby that Jesus saves. I saw more crosses than flags. And when I did see flags, they weren't always American flags. Confederate flags were hung on poles in front yards, displayed in the back window of a pickup truck, or as art on front license plates.

On our first full day in Kentucky, Sunday, we attended the local Baptist service. We arrived for 10 a.m. service to find out that we were an hour early. Sunday school was starting, and all seventy-three of us needed to make a decision.

Many of the youth elected to go to the children's Sunday school, while some adults took a drive through town. Having never attended Sunday school, I walked down the hall to the kitchen, joining the adults.

I was greeted warmly. A woman named Madonna, whose name alone implied so much more, approached me. She was the teacher. She introduced herself and asked my name.

"My name is Laura," I said. "I am here with the mission from Connecticut. My son is here too. It's our first mission trip, and first time to Kentucky."

Madonna welcomed me and walked to the front of the room.

There were a dozen or so of us seated there. I sipped on hot coffee while others nibbled on cake. It was a relaxed, yet focused atmosphere. I felt open, aware and welcomed.

I refer to myself as a recovering Catholic. I sat in the class and was struck not only by the level of intimacy that I felt, but also by how much I enjoyed it.

Madonna talked about clarity.

"You want to hear the message, not the messenger," she said. She talked about Biblical and modern-day people. Her message was strong and clear, a reminder to drop our egos. I had forgotten my reading glasses. Even at 52 years old, I am still in denial that I need them. I could not read along, so I listened, observed, and felt. Perhaps forgetting my reading glasses was the work of my ego.

I listened and watched her at the lectern. She went around the room and asked if there were any special prayers, intentions, or concerns. Many people shared personal challenges. Madonna asked us to keep them in our prayers.

A woman asked for healing prayers. Her husband, seated to her right, continued to battle cancer. They talked knowingly about a teenage girl who was a new mother and sent prayers to her. They agreed to collect money and baby supplies for her. The conversations were not hierarchical, but open and clear about need. Though they were talking about intimate details of this new mother's life, it did not sound gossipy. I felt genuine concern from the group. It was real and deeply personal.

I had never felt this way in a church before. These people were unfiltered and sharing their challenges. The lack of reading glasses kept me present, unable to look away or distract myself. The only thing different between me and these people were our accents.

And who has the accent, them or me? It depends who you ask.

After Sunday school, we filed into church. It was chatty, open and friendly. I felt like I was among family. In the row ahead of me, a seven-week old baby boy, Skyler, was held in his mother's arms. He occasionally gurgled and cooed, which made me smile.

The service was interactive. The pastor asked anyone who was interested to come to the altar to sing. About thirty people joined him, including Hudson. It felt uplifting and real in that Baptist church on that hot humid Sunday morning. The truth is, the whole morning — the Sunday school and the service — moved me to tears. I felt human kindness and caring in its simplest form. Individuals from all walks of life and different cultures found a common bond with each other. I looked at Hudson. He was smiling and singing.

The tears that started on Sunday did not end. I cried every day that week. I was moved by the contractor, Johnny Mullins from Homes, Inc. He shared local stories, and recounted the history of coal mining in the area. He told his story of growing up in eastern Kentucky. He even shared details about the night his son was born.

He told us of the Italian, Scottish, and Hungarian immigrants who moved in and worked the mines. How they'd arrived with nothing, and were set up with housing near the mines. They gave the workers credit that could only be used in the mine stores, to buy food and clothing. The early miner stories he shared told a story of slavery, of indentured servitude.

Johnny spoke in a slow, thick manner, occasionally turning his head away to spit brown liquid out of his mouth. A stout man with a sunburnt face, clear blue eyes, and endless patience, his walking and talking were deliberate. He was our contact person from Homes, Inc. Our group was divided up into work crews and assigned a Homes, Inc. representative. I believe we got the best one. He was a hard worker, knew his craft, and above all, was kind, friendly, and interested in getting to know us. After a week with Johnny, I understood why people stayed in eastern Kentucky. Their history and family pride was there.

Aside from Johnny, my work crew included Chet, a contractor from Connecticut, and four Branford High School students. We had no idea what our jobs were until we went to the site. There were a lot of lessons to be learned. Drinking water and seeking shade were obvious. The long days were hot and humid. Later in the week, we handled tin roofing. It was like carrying hot cookie sheets right out of the oven, without mitts.

The silver tin roofing had been delivered and was lying on the grass in neat stacks in the side yard, wrapped in plastic. Johnny instructed us to remove the packaging and stack the sheets according to size. The widths were always the same, but there were eight different lengths. The edges were sharp. We learned quickly to wear gloves. When we lifted individual pieces up, they rumbled like nearby thunder.

"Be careful not to scratch the surface," Johnny said. "It dings easy."

We learned a lot about taking direction, flexibility, respecting others, tools, and patience. Johnny was the lead contractor and he and Chet spoke another language. They spoke of bracing and right angles, and seemed to be constantly calculating. They would determine what needed to be done and assign tasks to each of the kids. They broke down these jobs step-by-step to avoid confusion. Their directions were clear and concise.

We worked on two homes that week. The first belonged to Connie and Daniel, a sister and brother. When we met them, they told us their father had built the house and raised twelve children in it. A single-story house, it was set into a nook at the base of a hill. The backyard was a narrow patch of grass that stepped up to a small stage-like landing. Three grave stones were there.

Connie said, "That's where our mother and daddy and one brother are buried."

Chet made a comment about how that would not be allowed where we live. There was serenity in the small cemetery. And I could not help but notice that the graves were well-tended with flower bouquets next to the gravestones.

The house was not as well-tended. There was mold and water damage and a general feeling of neglect. We arrived Monday morning to help complete the front deck and install new siding on either side of the front door.

There were multiple jobs to be completed. Chet and Stephen removed an old back window and installed a new one, while Erin caulked around the exterior of the living room window. Rob and Chris painted the new panels around the front door as well as the white molding. I did the least work. I kept the crew watered and fetched supplies as needed. I struggled with this role. I am a doer and attach a lot of my identity to getting things done. This idleness allowed me opportunities to talk with Johnny.

Talking came easy to Johnny, and at one point he referred to himself as a hillbilly. This came as a surprise to me, and I told him so.

"I would never call you a hillbilly," I said.

"Why not, that's what I am," he countered.

"It's a slur. It's a negative stereotype," I offered.

We talked about the origins of the word and about stereotypes and perceptions. We had different definitions and feelings about the word. Johnny looked at it as a description of a rural person. He talked about the way the television portrayed eastern Kentucky.

"They come here with an idea of what they want to see," he said. "They go looking for the worst of what we have here."

He shared this opinion with all of us. We nodded in agreement. What we had seen and read focused on the poverty and lack of opportunities. Johnny seemed to want to convey a deeper understanding of what life in eastern Kentucky was about. He conveyed this in the way he talked about northerners.

"We are country folk here, we live simply," he explained. "Northerners, or city folk, come here and think they know better." He told us about valuing a slower lifestyle, the beauty of the countryside and mountains, and the importance of community.

I asked him what the perception of northerners was.

"Some northerners come here and tell us the way things should be done, like we are stupid," he said. "Some northerners believe they are superior."

"This accent works against us," he said, smiling. "People hear this and assume we're ignorant. I can kind of see it, too. I wouldn't want a doctor talking country talk about a brain tumor to me."

I nodded and suggested that northerners prefer efficiency, wanting things to happen faster.

"We take into account your feelings when we speak," he said. "People from the north are blunt. Sometimes rude."

"Can you do a northern accent, Johnny?" I asked him.

He smiled, and thought about it.

"We see a lot of people from Michigan and Ohio here," he said. "There was a guy that worked with us from up there. He thought he knew better."

Standing over a sheet of tin roofing, Johnny put down the cutting shears.

"That's not how we do it up north," he said in a convincing northern accent.

I laughed and told him he nailed it — the accent, content, speed, and hubris.

I worked the least of the people on my crew. I had a lot of idle time between fetching water and tools from the back of Johnny's truck. In those quiet moments, I asked myself a question. What was I supposed to learn here? It had been more than two years since I dropped out of the corporate world. Since then, I have been seeking, searching for my life purpose. As the Buddha said, "your purpose in life is to find your purpose and give your whole heart and soul to it."

In the corporate world, I gave service to architects and interior designers with the intent of selling them a product. They gained and I gained. When I thought about the type of service that was given on a mission trip — helping others, service that matters deeply — the two experiences felt different. Both involved integrity and sincerity, so why did I feel different?

For years, I used my actions to provide clients with a good product and I benefitted by being paid for my ability to convince them of those features and benefits. My actions had a selfish motive.

In Kentucky, I understood the meaning of selflessness. I think that's why I cried every day. Our gestures and actions demonstrate our feelings in tangible ways; actions reveal the depth of who we are. Although Kentucky was wrought with generations of poverty, it was also a place of mystical beauty. The people and culture embodied this.

And as I seek my life purpose and allow myself to be transformed, the words of Leo Tolstoy remind me, "The sole meaning of life is to serve humanity."

Kentucky helped heal me; my tears were an emotional release. What I learned in Kentucky was about seeing beneath the surface, to what's important. It helped me see that my purpose in life was about serving.

CHAPTER 13

What Are You?

I was alone one Friday night; Hudson was spending the weekend with his dad. I did something I rarely do. I turned on the TV. Remote in hand, I clicked channel to channel, reaffirming why I never watch TV.

There was a man talking about tracking migration paths on the National Geographic program. I stopped clicking. He was retracing the steps of mankind's ancient ancestors. The images were beautiful, as he walked through Africa to the Middle East and onto Asia. At a commercial break, the announcer from Connecticut Public TV came on, appealing for donations. They were offering a connection to your past, a genome kit that would reveal your individual anthropological story.

I called the number on the screen, made my CPTV donation and gave them my address. The Geno 2.0 kit arrived soon after. Inside it had two swabs and two vials. Following the instructions, I swabbed the inside of both my cheeks and put the saliva tips into the vials. I sent the box off to the Genographic Project, to the scientists behind the research. I felt excited!

I was interested to learn about my deeper ancestry. As a fourth-generation American, I have grown used to, and annoyed by the question, "What are you?" When I first meet people and they hear my surname, Noe, "What are you?" is often the first question.

"I am a fourth-generation American," I answer.

"No, that's not what I mean. Where is Noe from?" they persist.

This is a frequently asked and widely accepted question in the U.S. When can I say American? Why must we cite recent ancestry? I can only go back to the 1700s, only 300 years ago.

Not very deep.

My irritation at the question is deeper. I feel it is an attempt to get a snapshot of what I am, to then apply stereotypes. For me, my shallow ancestry is, like a lot of Americans, a mix of many nationalities. If I were a dog, I would be a mutt. I have heard countless Americans describe themselves as mutts, a mix of breeds.

The thought of learning a deeper ancestry via the National Geographic genome project was compelling. Who were my ancestors before the 1700s, prior to Western Europe? The Geno 2.0 would track my DNA back 60,000 years. I could not wait for the results.

I tracked the progress of my DNA sample online. At a seemingly glacial pace, the results crept in — twenty-five percent complete, fifty percent complete. Until one morning, there it was. My deeper ancestry was revealed.

As excited as I had been to submit my saliva and await the results, when I read "completed" on the computer screen, I hesitated. Would my view of myself change? Would I feel differently as an American? What if I had, as two percent of the respondents do, Neanderthal roots? How would this information shift my view of my place in the world?

"Hudson! The results are in from National Geographic!" I yelled out. "Come in here and let's see this together!"

Hudson stood next to me as I clicked to the world map that would reveal 60,000 years of ancestry.

Starting in Sudan, the cradle of civilization, my ancestors migrated northeast to what is now Saudi Arabia. From there, the migration path continued north and east into Iran and Iraq. From the Middle East, my ancient family continued their migration up to

Scandinavia and Russia, and then into Western Europe.

It was powerful to see and know. Hudson and I smiled at each other. I thought about how Morocco had affected me. I was touched by the kindness of the people. Were my emotions linked to going "home?"

Perhaps every place we had been, we were meeting family members we didn't know. This thought made me feel connected to the world. And I realized, I am a citizen of the world.

The world is my family tree.

CHAPTER 14

Citizen of the World

"The world is my country and to do good is my religion."
— Thomas Paine

"It's not what you look at, it's what you see."
— Henry David Thoreau

The most important job I will ever have is being Hudson's mother. The travels we have experienced together have taught us both many things. About different cultures and religions, foods and lifestyles, architecture and interiors, customs, superstitions, communications, the way other people view the U.S. and Americans.

We have traveled to learn and explore new places and people. Upon return, we have new eyes and insights about our home. We want to be transformed, and return with our minds and hearts more open than when we left.

I believe it is important to expose him to different ways of living, with hopes of cultivating empathy, understanding, and open-mindedness in him. I want him to become the best person he can be. I want to cultivate curiosity, wonder, and amazement about the world.

I want him to grow into a man who has purpose. I want him to find his passion. I want him have relationships and connections, take chances, believe in himself and his dreams. I want him to not make money his primary pursuit.

We are reminded daily of our interconnectedness. I feel it is important for Hudson to learn this empirically — to go, see, and taste the world. Not just read about it. Do it. It is important for him to learn to be a verb and take action.

My goal is selfish. I am a mother, not a martyr. I want to go, see, and taste the world as well. I am raising a citizen of the world. Each of our trips has started the same way. Looking at a map, asking questions, and pausing to acknowledge how lucky we are to be able to live this way.

Though each of our trips has been different, they all end the same. We return home, with an abundance of new, life-altering memories. The pictures remind us of the stories and experiences that have brought my son and me closer. Our time together has been well spent, educational, and inspiring.

We know so little about the world, and want to learn more. When I consider the benefits of traveling with my son, I am of two minds — the human and the mother mind. They do intersect. My hopes include cultivating awareness in my son to lift his eyes above Branford, and Connecticut, and the United States. I want his eyes lifted way up, to see the whole world.

The experiences and exposure to what was and what wasn't happening in Turkey was a lesson in discernment. It taught Hudson to think, to evaluate, and to look below the surface of what was being reported by the media.

While the benefits *for* a child to travel are numerous, the benefits traveling *with* a child are equally profound. Spending time together has been a bonding experience. Spending time in environments that are foreign to both of us brings us closer. We animatedly talk about places and culture, local politics and lifestyle, food and beliefs, perceptions and stereotypes. Our conversations are thoughtful, fueled by exposure to newness away from our everyday routine. My mind has been reinvigorated by our trips.

We ask questions. We are curious. Some of the questions and musings are ones we would have never thought to ask. Like the ones about toilets and indoor plumbing.

Hudson has been the catalyst on our trips. He has shaped the experiences we have had. Traveling with another adult, I would not have eaten the donut in Český Krumlov, or spontaneously dropped my suitcase to go whitewater rafting. With Hudson's urging, we went to a carnival in Paris and rode a Ferris wheel at sunset, moved by the lights and beauty of Sacré-Cœur.

I am the adult, the one in charge, discerning what we will and won't do. But it has been Hudson's openness and joie de vivre that have had a halo effect on me. He teaches me. I get to let loose, be spontaneous and silly. And I learn. My love of travel has been enhanced by Hudson. He keeps it real. We experience life as it is happening, not making plans too far out.

I dropped out of the competitive corporate world for many reasons. My core values did not match the corporate world anymore. I value people more than profits. My meaning, my purpose in life, is to strive to be the best person I can be. That includes being the best mother, keeping my priorities straight.

During one of my many corporate trips, I called Hudson on the phone to catch up on his day. At the end of the conversation, he said, "I feel like I am having mom withdrawal." On the other end of the line, my eyes watered. I had a lump in my throat as I croaked out, "I miss you too, honey. I will be home soon."

When I reflect on that moment, and the power of his words on me, I understand and feel most what it is to be a mother. That meant priorities and presence. Re-examining my own core values. Leaving the golden-handcuffed corporate life was easy, as his words gave me clarity.

A common desire among parents is that we want things to be better for our kids than they were for us. There are many stories illustrating how hard that wish is becoming. My wishes for Hudson are not about buying a house and a car. My wish for him is to be a part — an active part — of the world. Help other people, serve, reach out, appreciate what and who you have, leave people and places better than you found them, and to be his own person.

I want him to regard the world as his family, as traveling the world with him has taught me.

We always have choice. Some of the most important choices I make are about the values I want my son to grow up with. Among those values that I want to impart to him are perceptions about time and money.

I have read countless stories about people who have looked back on their lives with regret. They wish they had done things differently. Often, the remorse is in the way they spent their time. They spent a lot of time working and less time living.

These stories resonate with me because I have floated in and out of the corporate world for years. The "in" years brought me a lot of money and benefits and afforded me opportunities to make choices on how I spent my money. In the earlier years, I spent it on material things — homes, clothes, and stuff that needed dusting. During those years I was on a treadmill. The mantra: Faster is better.

The off years were slower; I started a consulting business and made choices. How I spent my time and money shifted. I no longer wanted to amass material things. I chose to use my time and money on experiences. Spending time with children is more important than spending money on them.

Often, the best things in life are the hardest. Vacation is for relaxing. The word is a noun meaning a person, place, or a thing. Vacations are for resting. It's what you go on when your life is packed, busy, and allows no time for respite.

We travel. Travel is a verb. Travel implies action, movement, transformation in place as well as perspective. Occasionally there may be some relaxing, but overall, when we return from travel, I need a vacation. I would have it no other way.

Culturally, and as a species, we desire comfort. I feel when people stay too long in the comfort, it breeds staleness and depression, boredom, complacency and entitlement. Our culture places a lot of emphasis and value on ease and speed. When we travel, both these concepts disappear, as everywhere else in the world, life is harder and slower. And it is wonderful.

This idea of authenticity is also something I want to expose Hudson to. Our society is increasingly synthetic — people, things, food — so much of it rooted in perfectionism and narcissism. I want Hudson to care, really care, about people and buck the "if it's not happening to me, it doesn't matter" mindset.

My behavior is fueled by belief. A belief in values that are inclusive and democratic, because when you strip away the race, religion and/or class, the divine DNA is all the same. As Mark Twain said, "Travel is fatal to prejudice, bigotry and narrow-mindedness." Trust, belief, and faith are important to being a mother.

I have to trust that I have instilled good values into my son. Paradoxically, I know that suffering will make him into a better, more empathic, understanding man. Knowing he will amass scar tissue is difficult. I love him; I don't want him to suffer. However, I know the comfort cocoon will not serve him. And neither would my enabling.

How can I instill solid core values within my son? How do I cultivate humbleness when he is a white American boy growing up in Connecticut? What is his purpose? The answer is found in discomfort.

To cultivate humbleness, he must experience discomfort, settings, situations and people that challenge his comfort zone. I challenge my comfort zone by taking classes, meeting new people, volunteering, saying yes more than no, being vulnerable, and asking questions. I expect less and learn more. I achieve this by traveling with him.

Through new experiences, we both are made uncomfortable. That is where the humble confidence is formed. With every new experience, my trust is challenged and I ask myself one question: What If?

The question is impossible to avoid, it is a measurement, a barometer and ultimately a question of faith and trust. I asked this question constantly as we traveled.

Fear will not rule my life. Fear will not rule my thoughts or actions.

My behavior has been fueled by a belief that the best thing will happen. The best possible outcome will be our experience. It has been with that optimistic attitude that I prevail. I have been able to experience life with him with greater confidence. If something goes wrong, I look at it as a learning opportunity. I do not equate snafus with fear.

When I reflect on travels with my son, I see how far we have come together. We started safe, on the east coast, close to home. Gradually, we built our confidence, left the country and crossed the Atlantic Ocean multiple times.

Traveling has helped me see.

After dinner one night, Hudson and I took Chase for a walk up to the Branford green. We talked about future trip ideas. We stopped to let Chase sniff a fire hydrant. Hudson looked at me and said, "Mom, when I grow up and have kids, I am going to travel with them."

Acknowledgements

We stand on each other's shoulders. And I am only as smart as the people who have come before me. The support, guidance, and encouragement I have received while writing this book has enabled me to bring this project to fruition. If I have had a conversation with you, then you have helped inform me on the opinions and insights in this book. Everyone has a story and every story is compelling. I have loved listening to and benefitting from your perspectives. Though I have operated on a global scale, my village is mighty and is deserving of recognition.

My son, Hilliard Hudson Wolfe, who arrived full-bodied and robust on September 8, 1999, continually teaches and inspires me. I am proud of him daily. For my friends who fanned my flame, fed me verbal vitamins, and kept my faith alive, I give thanks to: Susan Kissel, Barbara Meehan, and Jean Fitzsimmons.

I give thanks also to my first draft readers, Theresa Borchetta, Margaret Thompson, Georgette Wood, and Donna D'Amico. To Wick Wolfe, Hudson's dad. To John Wolfe and Adrianna Wheelock, my stepson and stepdaughter, who taught me how to be a mom. To the nine women in my writing group for their openness, guidance, and honesty. To Millie Calesky for teaching me to mind map and for her coaching insights. To John Weinstein at Adler Travel for helping us select and plan our journeys. To Kim MacQueen and Cindy Barnes for their editing and writing suggestions and belief in this project. My worldview is shaped and expanded by everyone I meet. Thank you.

www.ingramcontent.com/pod-product-compliance
Lightning Source LLC
Chambersburg PA
CBHW051943290426
44110CB00015B/2087